Governing through Technology

Technology, Work and Globalization

The Technology, Work and Globalization series was developed to provide policy makers, workers, managers, academics and students with a deeper understanding of the complex interlinks and influences between technological developments, including information and communication technologies, work organizations and patterns of globalization. The mission of the series is to disseminate rich knowledge based on deep research about relevant issues surrounding the globalization of work that is spawned by technology.

Also in the series:

Governing through Technology

Information Artefacts and Social Practice

Jannis Kallinikos

Professor, Information Systems and Innovation Group, Department of Management, London School of Economics and Political Science

First published 2011 by
PALGRAVE MACMILLAN

Palgrave Macmillan in the UK is an imprint of Macmillan Publishers Limited, registered in England, company number 785998, of Houndmills, Basingstoke, Hampshire RG21 6XS.

Palgrave Macmillan in the US is a division of St Martin's Press LLC, 175 Fifth Avenue, New York, NY 10010.

Palgrave Macmillan is the global academic imprint of the above companies and has companies and representatives throughout the world.

Palgrave® and Macmillan® are registered trademarks in the United States, the United Kingdom, Europe and other countries

ISBN 978–0–230–28088–5   hardback

This book is printed on paper suitable for recycling and made from fully managed and sustained forest sources. Logging, pulping and manufacturing processes are expected to conform to the environmental regulations of the country of origin.

A catalogue record for this book is available from the British Library.

A catalog record for this book is available from the Library of Congress.

10 9 8 7 6 5 4 3 2 1
20 19 18 17 16 15 14 13 12 11

Printed and bound in Great Britain by
CPI Antony Rowe, Chippenham and Eastbourne

To my parents, in memoriam

Contents

List of Tables

List of Figures

Foreword

With Bakhtin we can agree that all dialogues are unfinished. Though there is no end in sight, some turns in the current of conversation change and reward us in unusually satisfying ways. New vistas and openings reanimate discussion with insightful and, sometimes, disquieting perceptions and comprehensions. Jannis Kallinikos's *Governing through Technology: Information Artefacts and Social Practice* is such a turn. A rare thoughtfulness, care, analytical sharpness and breadth of vision infuse every page of this book.

I first became aware of Kallinikos's work in 2006 when I happened across the trenchant 'Farewell to Constructivism: Technology and Context-embedded Action' (Kallinikos, 2004c). In this essay, Kallinikos argues that situated studies of local activity misapprehend contemporary technologies and technological systems such as nuclear power, highways and large information systems. These systems are neither negotiable nor configurable in meaningful ways as suggested by concepts of situatedness; they do not admit of personal choice, or selective engagement based on individual preferences.

I found this observation particularly interesting since my professional community of American informatics subscribes enthusiastically to notions of 'user control', 'malleability', 'personalization', 'customization', 'adaptive interfaces' and so on, as significant markers of our relations to digital technologies. A reading of Kallinikos's paper shows that no matter how well intentioned, such notions mislead. They circumscribe (as Kallinikos helps us see) our field of vision to 'users' confronting devices or software programs.

In his precise, economical way, Kallinikos (2004c) asserts the problematic nature of such a position, making the critical point that construals of technology

> cannot be exhausted at the very interface upon which humans encounter technology. Essential strips of reality are not observable or even describable at the level of contextual encounters.

It is the heroic undertaking of *Governing through Technology* to enable us to progress towards more cogent means of observing and describing those 'essential strips of reality'. Kallinikos approaches this vital project with several tricks up his sleeve, or perhaps I should say artfully managed intellectual techniques. These techniques are deployed in the service of producing a book that is genuinely *useful*, offering a set of bold, carefully worked claims that aid the reader in transcending comforting but vague, and even ill-considered, notions of technological self-efficacy, and somewhat blurry concepts and assumptions suggesting the equivalence of technology and practice.

Kallinikos's first technique is to urge us to re-examine our invocation of terms such as 'negotiate' to indicate relations between social practice and technology. While evocative, we apply these terms (others that come to mind are 'mutually constitute', 'interpenetrate' and 'entangle') loosely, not knowing quite what we mean by them. They carry pleasing connotations of flexibility and interconnection, and we turn to them to critique rigid notions of technological determinism. We certainly feel better for having done so, but what, in the end, do we mean?

'Negotiation', for example, as Kallinikos observes, denotes a relation in which two or more parties with divided interests attempt to come to terms with one another. Even setting aside the precarious notion of a human negotiating with say, an Enterprise Resource Planning (ERP) system, to use one of Kallinikos's analytical objects, a more serious complication lies in the way this rendering presupposes two distinct, separable entities, independently formed. Kallinikos argues that humans (or their social practices) cannot be seen thus; they are, in part, unmistakably *products of technologies*. As he succinctly puts it: 'Technology is not exogenous to human agency, as the contrast of humans to machines may initially suggest.'

Kallinikos develops concrete instantiations of this claim. For example, our professional skill sets arise as a direct outcome of the technologies with which we do our work. One does not have to look far to find resumes cheerfully boasting 'Skills': Java, C++, XML, UML, Rational Rose! The software engineer whose résumé is thus assembled has hardly entered into negotiations with these technical languages and platforms; he has assimilated them, and they have become, in critical ways, who he is, instrumentally with respect to the functions he can perform at work, and in his very identity as someone skilled at applying them. A notion of negotiation then, in which separate parties square off trading points of divided interest, misses a fundamental reality in which technologies cultivate and bring forth our selves, rather than standing apart from those selves. Throughout the book, Kallinikos administers the gentle but firm technique of prompting us to say or think what we mean as we speak of negotiation, and so on, to construe the human relation to technology.

A second technique Kallinikos mobilizes, perhaps less gently and with more force, is to insist on positioning questions of technology in a wide historical purview. This strategy is imperative for foundational theoretical reasons: contemporary technologies, especially digital technologies, are interlinked over vast spatial scales, and each is the outcome of lengthy historical processes. The linkages and processes are broad and deep; their nature is revealed only when analysis occurs at appropriate temporal and spatial scales. Linkages and processes 'penetrate deep down into the social fabric', as Kallinikos says, and produce, in part, the micro-order of social practice. If we turn away from analysing them, we can never hope to achieve knowledge of practice that extends very far beyond limited, ahistorical accounts.

Framed in another way, Kallinikos's advocacy of historical analysis is a technique to argue for change in intellectual practice. He observes that the instrumental bias of research in organizational studies, information science, computer science and management studies leads us towards detailed investigations of particular technologies (in the hopes of deploying them more effectively) and away from broad questions about technology that have been raised at least since Plato's time. In the current context, we are reluctant to deliberate on 'technology in the singular', and so we dumb down, in a way, issues of *techne* by busying ourselves observing particular technologies in local contexts, and the infinite twists and turns they offer up to our gaze. Furthermore, the 'complex and time-evolving' patterns that comprise Praxis, which we should aim to grasp, yield to smaller studies of practice. Academic silos exacerbate the situation; which 'department' is in charge of the big picture?

A third technique, pursuant to the second, is to place before us, throughout the book, the Question that Will Not Go Away. Although we may feel sure that we have beaten the technological determinism horse to death, Kallinikos reminds us that the 'regulative regime' of technology is alive and well. We cannot avoid it in discussions invoking memes such as 'code is law', video-game addiction, the ubiquity of hacking, cognitive and social dangers of multitasking with our arrays of digital technologies, the advent of 'CrackBerries'. Such rhetoric – necessary, it seems, in light of the experiences we are having with digital technologies – is not intended to resurrect simple causal schemes of 'the technology made me do it' variety, but appears in the discourse as a result of the powerful shapings technology entrains. It is incumbent upon us to examine these shapings and their undeniable presence in our lives.

A fourth technique, and perhaps one that sets Kallinikos's analyses apart from some other ambitious treatments, is that the *human person* is always present. Analysis at scale is capable of preserving the person, offering understandings complementary to those obtained when the level of abstraction begins at the organization or network. In reading *Governing through Technology*, though we are immersed in difficult questions concerning the properties of huge technological systems cast in highly abstract terms, we are never actually far from the people enmeshed in these systems. Kallinikos's portrayal of the workers in the Scandinavian dairy processing plant struggling to understand the computer printouts that are supposed to govern their work is an unforgettable image. The superlative contribution of the book is to enable us to see the workers in a complex historical system stretching from the local work group in the dairy, to the plant, to the dairy and global software industries that impose the necessity of the printouts and everything they encumber. Within this broad scope, Kallinikos addresses the 'strips of reality' that form the person: skill-making, the mediation of reality and identity-building.

Casting his eye down this line of sight, Kallinikos draws on art as well as science to weave his special web. For it is a web indeed; once within we can no longer be satisfied confusing or conflating social structure and technology, collapsing crucial categories to avoid the daunting task of understanding the grounds upon which they must be distinguished from one another. Kallinikos responds to the enormity of this task with a formidable ensemble of tools: logic, theory, rigorous empirical study, a deep reading of multiple literatures and art. He concludes *Governing through Technology* with an excursion to Italo Calvino's *Invisible Cities*. Herein Marco Polo and Kublai Khan enter into an epic chess game out of which Kallinikos adroitly derives understandings of the ways in which the representations and abstractions of digital technology alter, and, in some cases, shrink and distort 'the plenitude of reality', as Kallinikos estimably calls it, through the specific, particular properties of the technology. Such a manoeuvre, that is, invoking a dense literary metaphor, is a final technique, to afford us, the readers, another mode in which to discern the complex questions with which Kallinikos contends. Above all, *Governing through Technology* is a generous book; Kallinikos holds himself to very high standards of precision of thought and expressiveness from which the engaged reader profits immensely.

Governing through Technology: Information Artefacts and Social Practice is a decisive turn in the unfinished dialogue regarding technology and practice. That the dialogue stretches back centuries bespeaks its enduring importance and the 'wicked problems' it insinuates into our attempts to understand who we are. About these wicked problems Kallinikos has much to say. Some peaceful hours of quiet (perhaps stolen from the very technologies that Kallinikos writes about so perceptively), devoted to this remarkable book, will repay study many times over.

Bonnie Nardi
Department of Informatics, University of California, Irvine

1
Technology as Object of Social Enquiry

Introduction

From the range of loosely connected ideas we pursue in our intellectual life, occasionally some may converge into a common cause. Suddenly or progressively, works that appeared unconnected disclose an underlying pattern. Such is this volume, made up of a few previously published pieces that span a range of topics. The affinities these writings share were suggested to me along the way. Each project we carry out often shows old ones in a new light. As part of this volume, the original publications have been revised, some less, others more substantially. In revising them, I have sought to make their affinities clearer and to demonstrate the links connecting the ideas I pursue.

The thread that is spun throughout the chapters concerns the interrelationship between information technology and social practice, and the institutional contexts within which social practice is articulated and embedded. The pursuit of this theme takes place against the awareness of the increasing significance which technological information acquires in shaping perception, communication and action patterns, at work or otherwise. By technological information, I mean semantic or cultural content (text, sound, image) produced and disseminated by technological and considerably automated means. A recurrent motif therein is how technology and human agency have an impact on one another. These themes are certainly contentious and recurrent. For the scholar that knows the contingent and ambiguous nature of social life, the attempt to relate the making of institutions and agency forms to technological processes may well summon the spectres of determinism and reductionism that have haunted social enquiry ever since its inception. At the same time, the themes are recurrent and indicative, I think, of the wider recognition that human agency and institutions are variously entangled with the object world and the various supports which its solidity and stability grants to social life. This may appear to be a Foucauldian motif and it may well be. But it has deeper and diverse roots within social science and philosophy (e.g., Adorno, 1973, 1984; Valéry, 1989; Winnicott, 1971).

The claims I make throughout the volume suggest that technology is variously implicated in the constitution of the objectives of social action and the agency forms by which these objectives are sought. By agency forms, I mean institutionally anchored ways or models of acting and communicating that may range from entrenched professional or occupational profiles and organizational roles to less formal, yet culturally embedded, modes of conduct. I also make a case for the fact that technology participates in the building of many of the institutional scaffolds (organizations, structural arrangements and practices) within which social objectives and agency forms impact upon one another. These outcomes are not achieved solely by virtue of the interpretive frame and the conventions that develop around the functions and uses of technological artefacts or systems (e.g., Bijker, 2001). They also owe a great deal, as architecture manifestly shows, to the material forms on which they lean and the reified functions these forms help to summon (Lessig, 2006).

These may appear to be bold claims. It is legitimate to raise concerns as to the role technology plays in human affairs and question whether it can have other than a limited role in shaping social objectives and agency forms. Academics and lay people hold a widespread belief that technology is a means to the service of human ends, a passive, as it were, universe of objects whose functions and purposes are summoned and enacted in the ongoing pursuits of humans and the contexts within which these pursuits occur. True as this may sound, it nonetheless reflects just one side of a much more complex and variegated picture. Artefacts *qua* means are never neutral. They make some things possible and exclude others. Artefacts embody values or 'have politics', as Langdon Winner (1986) poignantly reminds us. Furthermore, in societies such as ours, artefacts seldom stand alone. They often belong to larger technical assemblages or networks that orchestrate human pursuits, mediating our relationship with the world in non-trivial ways. Indeed, many of the dominant technologies of our age assume the form of extended networks (highway or rail traffic, broadcasting, telephony, energy distribution, the Internet) in which extensive and varying operational connections and functional dependencies prevail.

But there is more to it. Technology is not exogenous to human agency, as the contrast of humans to machines may initially suggest. Technology does not constitute a force that simply has to be used, resisted, bypassed or altogether avoided; although these things admittedly happen. In being an indispensable part of human pursuits, technology contributes to constructing forms of agency by shaping skill profiles and professional practices over time (Kallinikos & Hasselbladh, 2009; Kallinikos, Hasselbladh & Marton, 2010). Particularly in the current situation in which information artefacts penetrate every walk of life, technology becomes a central element in the construction of the micro-order of daily working and living. The facilities it provides embody a variety of routines and procedures at the same time as they generate a range of perceptual and cognitive stimuli that influence human behaviour in many subtle ways (Borgmann, 1999; Manovich, 2001). Finally, artefacts and technologies frequently become status objects and the medium and target of personal affect and identification. The Internet furnishes a polyvalent medium and potent example of all these processes of skill-making, reality mediation and identity-building.

Information as epistemic category

In today's world, the overwhelming majority of objects that populate our lives are indeed technological or, at least, technologically derived. I am concerned here, however, not with objects as such but with that subset of objects that are used to construct or modify other objects or produce, as in the case of heating or television, a change in the immediate environment of one's living. I confine the term 'technology' to such *generative* or *interactive* artefacts and refer to the rest as objects. The distinction is admittedly blurred in many contexts, however, it does have the merit of directing attention towards the ongoing loop of interactions through which technological affordances are enacted and the greater leeway they thus obtain by becoming implicated in human affairs.

Among the various technologies that populate modern life, I am particularly concerned in this volume with that smaller, yet steadily expanding, subset of systems or artefacts deployed to process, store and communicate information. The subset therefore comprises all computer-based systems and the connecting ecologies their links establish both at the local level and in the wider environment that is currently marked by the ubiquitous presence of the Internet. Information technologies are of particular importance for the simple reason that they massively introduce machine-based processing of information and its communication across work and community life.

Prior to the advent of computing machines, information processing and communication had firmly remained the prerogative of humans, no matter how extensively these tasks may have been aided by a range of mnemonic or signal-transmitting devises.

Information is an epistemic category, providing the cognitive means on the basis of which reality is described, known, changed, augmented or supplanted (as in virtual states). I therefore refer to information as a *semantic phenomenon*. In this respect, information is a subset of culture even when natural signs are interpreted as carrying information, that is, cloud or thunder signifying rain. Such a definition excludes information from natural or biological phenomena that are often described as entailing information processing (see Bateson, 1972; Borgmann, 1999). Information as semantic content can be seen as the upper level of the technological complex that marks our age, supported from below by automated means of processing syntactic tokens (i.e., the software) and the hardware infrastructure on which these processes are wired (Benkler, 2006). It is characteristic of our age and indicative of the problems I focus on here that these levels intersect one another at several points (Kallinikos, 2009a).

The embodiment of information processing onto software machines that constitute the middle layer of this technological complex marks an important turning point in the history of technology that has up to the emergence of computers been predominantly concerned with the duplication and manipulation of physical and locomotive processes (Simon, 1969; Zuboff, 1988). Communication by means of technical media (telegraph and telephone) and office technologies (e.g., the typewriter, numerical machines) certainly preceded the advent of computing machines and can indeed be seen as the predecessors of computers and computer technology (Beniger, 1986; Winston, 1998; Yates, 1989). Yet, computer-mediated information processing and communication are different in the sense that they embody in the machine a version of what is believed to be human or animal intelligence, what at the very bottom constitutes the 'magic', as Kevin Turner calls it, of software.[1]

Through information and information processing, technology interferes with thinking processes affecting perception, recall and memory and, more widely, cognition (Ekbia, 2008; Kallinikos, 1995, 1998). Critical facets of reality are approached, sampled and comprehended through the cognitive blocks and processes provided by an interlinked ecology of information

---

[1] Kevin Turner in a public talk at the London School of Economics, 3 February 2010. Mr Turner is Chief Operating Officer of Microsoft Corporation.

artefacts and operations. This occurs through the arrangement and packaging of the cultural content with which humans interact but also, and, crucially, through automated processes of information processing (varieties of software) well beyond the awareness, perceptual ability or skill of humans. As these trends diffuse throughout the social fabric, information grows to a comprehensive perceptual and cognitive net, a complex grid used to segment and assemble reality for the purpose of describing, transforming and, even as occurs increasingly today, replacing it altogether with the surrogate reality versions it disseminates (Borgmann, 1999).[2] Information and the technologies by which it is produced and distributed are also important means of communication. Computer-mediated communication entails an exchange of messages under conditions in which the contextual details of meaning are often missing and must increasingly be imagined and filled in by those involved in communication (Bateson, 1972; Esposito, 2004).[3]

If this is a valid picture then the impact these developments have upon social practice cannot but be far reaching. By social practice I do not mean community life or recurring patterns of social interaction but mostly institutionalized spheres of expertise that occur either in formal organizations and/or in collective forms known as 'professions' (Freidson, 2001; Tsivacou, 2003). The line separating the latter from the former may not always be clear (Schatzki, Knorr-Cetina & Von Savingy, 2001) but I think most often it is. Regrettably the study of these wider implications of information and the forms it is implicated in institutional change is either neglected or pursued without due attention to detail, as often happens in macro-sociological studies of information and information technologies (e.g., Castells, 1996; Poster, 1990, 2006).[4]

A widely diffused belief, closely associated with the pre-eminence of the user in contemporary computer design, portrays interaction with information-based systems and artefacts as far more malleable and adaptable to diverse human pursuits than traditional, materially embedded technologies. In the place of the unresponsive character of material artefacts,

---

[2]See the 8th SSIT on 'The Habitat of Information', held at the London School of Economics, Spring 2008, http://www.lse.ac.uk/collections/informationSystems/newsAndEvents/2008events/SSIT8.htm. Accessed on 10 August 2010.
[3]Even in the simple case of mobile phone or Skype conversations the context of the person one is speaking with has to be gradually assembled from various cues including the conversation itself in order to provide a fuller understanding of the verbal exchange.
[4]There are of course exceptions, see, for example, Crozier (2007, 2009) and Esposito (2011).

information-based artefacts allow for various degrees of interactivity and the handling of contingencies that mark contemporary life. While this is perhaps true, such a belief must be qualified to take into account the wider grid of relations into which information and the technologies supporting it are embedded that I mentioned briefly above. The nature of information-based technologies as technologies of cognition suggests that they become entangled in human affairs in a much more penetrating and complex fashion. A simple operation on one's desktop draws on a variety of software programs many of which may be distributed over the Web (Kallinikos, Aaltonen & Marton, 2010; Manovich, 2001). As these technologies diffuse, they mingle with human pursuits in various ways that are difficult to disentangle. The same flexibility of computing technologies that allows adaptation to specific contexts and contingencies opens up a wider corridor through which the operations of technologies conflate with those of humans. There is no better evidence of this than the increasing infiltration of daily life by the artefacts and processes of the technologies of computing and communication.[5]

The writings that make up this volume are not, however, derived from the texture of everyday living. They have emerged rather from concerns that relate to the institutional matrix of relations in which these technologies are embedded. Although the empirical facts reported here are limited to a couple of chapters, the majority of writings have grown out of empirical projects involving the investigation of public agencies and corporations (see, e.g., Contini & Lanzara, 2009; Kallinikos & Mariategui, 2008) and the influence technologies have on the making of the institutional fabric (Kallinikos, 2006). They are concerned mostly with institutional relations rather than with individuals or individual perception and the use of technology in community life. They accordingly draw on several disciplines such as workplace sociology, social studies of science and technology, organization studies, information theory, semiotics and communication theory and information-systems research. They are also informed by wider philosophical currents on technology and the cultural schemes of reality mediation (representation) and communication with which information-based technologies are closely associated.[6]

The cross-fertilization of the contingent pursuits of empirical enquiry with the wider and more enduring concerns of philosophy and art theory is a challenging task whose outcome is highly uncertain. But this is what

---

[5] For instance, handheld computers, camcorders, other handsets such as ipods, ipads or mobile phones.

[6] See Borgmann (1999), Eco (1976), Goodman (1976, 1978), Flusser (2000, 2002), Mumford (1934, 1952) and Sontag (1979).

animates the present writings, giving them their distinctive flavour. In many respects, the growth and increasing involvement of the technologies of computing and communication in social life and the diffusion of the Internet demonstrate the inadequacy and limits of the prevailing academic division of labour. I do not think it possible to account for the social and economic implications of the developments I describe here without venturing to cross disciplinary boundaries in non-trivial ways. The task is complex, subtle and demanding and, not surprisingly, has few adherents in the well-insulated enclosures of contemporary academia.

The structure of the book

Following these introductory remarks, Chapter 2, 'The Regulative Regime of Technology', describes technology as an important regulative force of social practice. Technology is distinguished from *social structure* (role differentiation) and *culture* (norm-building) as the two other major regulative regimes that have shaped institutions and social practice in modern times. Being the offspring of culture in a historical sense, technology might appear strange to separate from it. The claim I make to support such an analytic distinction is that it pays to distinguish technology, social structure and culture on the basis of the emphasis they place on the object–subject continuum as the primary medium/target for shaping and governing behaviour. Thus, technology obtains its distinctive regulative reach thanks to the variety of *strategies of functional simplification* and *reification* by which it lays out its prescriptive order. Technology just works through extensive reification (objectification), that is, the embodiment of agency onto technical objects and systems. Thus conceived, it differs from social structure and the latter's heavy reliance on *formal role systems* and the *differentiation of roles* and *duties* (e.g., hierarchy) and culture that relies primarily on *the interiorization of norms* and *action patterns* as the key modality of forging legible and accountable patterns of action.

Chapter 3, 'Bounds and Freedoms: Re-opening the Blackbox of Technology', pursues further some of these issues against the widespread belief that posits the emergent, use-driven attributes of technologies as evidence of the blank or void, as it were, nature of technology and its infinite malleability. In distancing myself from this position, I seek to construct an analytic map on which to place the variability of information-based artefacts and the way they are involved in shaping agency forms. Drawing on Nelson Goodman's (1976, 1978) cognitive philosophy, I adopt his distinction of *score*, *script* and *sketch*, and deploy it as the conceptual tool for disentangling the composite nature of items and relations underlying the constitution of cognition-based technological artefacts. The key insight to be derived from Goodman's framework is that each of these three basic cultural types summons different forms of agency, consequent upon the ways in which they parse and reassemble the reality they address. While the score admits interpretation, it provides a well-trodden path (a sequence of clearly defined steps of the notational system of music) along which to execute performance of a piece of music and, in this quality, it contrasts sharply with the sketch (drawing) which mediates a compact depiction of a target domain but lacks the stipulation of a clear path with respect to how sketching is to be accomplished.[7] The separation of agency from the means on which it relies remains implicit in the case of the sketch, whereas it is more elaborate and differentiated in the case of the score. The script (verbal writing) lies somewhere between the two. Such an analysis is used as a basis for inferring the malleability and negotiability of software-based technologies and the forms by which they admit human involvement and participation.

Chapter 4, 'Unpacking Information Packages: Rationalization and Governance', moves to the empirical domain of large-scale information systems known as Enterprise Resource Planning (ERP) or Enterprise systems and provides an illustration of some of the claims put forth in the preceding chapters. The organizational involvement of such systems, I argue, has important implications that go far beyond the acknowledged motif of maintaining the integration of organizational operations across functions and production sites. The chapter shows in some detail that packages of this sort encode a logic of action that is embedded in the prescriptive structure of data items and the relationships these bear with one another. Owing to the inclusive character of these packages, that logic becomes both the standardized receptacle of inputs and the springboard on the basis of which operations are instrumented, conducted and monitored. While cast in the appropriate rhetoric of market adaptation, 'best practice' and 're-engineering', the diffusion of such packages recounts the drastic simplification of organizations as institutions in which the distribution and carrying out of duties traditionally reflects a variety of modes of involvement and a multifaceted assembly of experiences, skills and preoccupations.

Chapter 5, 'Addendum on the Behavioural Implications of Information Packages', further pursues the critical deconstruction of ERP packages and the model of human agency the prescriptive nature of these packages disseminates. Work roles and duties are instrumented as procedural sequences to be carried out by relying on the package orchestration of the steps,

---

[7] The difference is akin to that between digital and analogue systems.

substeps and items by which a certain task or series of tasks is conceived as being made. I show, in some detail, that such a conception of work duties recounts a very specific and, in a sense, limited understanding of humans and organizations. This becomes evident in the juxtaposition of the models of human agency ERP packages embody with other and habitual forms of human action that entail the ongoing testing of one's behaviour against environmental cues, renegotiation and rerouting. These latter forms of human involvement stand out against the serial fragmentation underlying procedural action. They imply acting upon the world on loose premises that trade off a variety of forms of knowledge and courses of action in attempts to explore and discover alternative ways of coping with reality.

Chapter 6, 'Control and Complexity in a Connected World', seeks to establish the link between technology and organization form, and assess the organizational impact of the current developments associated with the growing involvement of information technologies in organizations and the diffusion of the Internet. Extending the analysis undertaken in Chapter 2, and drawing on Luhmann (1993, 1995), traditional forms of technological control are analysed in terms of functional simplification and closure. Functional simplification entails the demarcation of an operational domain within which the complexity of the world is reconstructed as a simplified set of tight cause-and-effect couplings. Functional closure implies the construction of a protective cocoon that is placed around the cause–effects sequences to fence off contingencies and ensure their recurrent unfolding. Technology, in the traditional forms of mass production or process industries, epitomizes this logic and has been a key means for separating technical operations from social roles. At the same time, it has furnished the model for designing organizations as bounded systems of clear-cut tasks and well-demarcated roles. Contemporary technologies of computing and communication are, by and large, premised on the same model, yet they introduce a crucial shift consisting of the commensurability and linking of the technological solutions they provide and the concomitant undermining of the closure principle. The deepening connectivity of software-based technologies and the diffusion of the Internet provide a clear indicator of this commensurable technological space in which technologies and artefacts are possible to link to greater ecologies or systems. These developments carry both novel risks and opportunities. They also reorganize the infrastructural basis on which bounded systems have relied and promote alternative forms of organization often subsumed under the notion of 'network'.

Chapter 7, 'Cognitive Foundations of Work: The Workplace as Information', is a study of the cognitive transformation of work consequent upon the diffusion of information tokens and the rendering of information to the key cognitive currency by means of which workplace processes and relations are perceived, instrumented and controlled. The development and use of various symbol systems for representing, recording, indexing and processing information has been widely diffused in modern times, for example, finance, accounting and auditing and library science. However, the deepening embedment of computer-based technologies in organizations marks an important shift that establishes information tokens a pervasive element of workplace steering and control. As information diffuses throughout the workplace, it makes the problem of extracting meaning from the pervasive and often technical cognitive texture the use of software packages generates endemic. These ideas are further elaborated in the empirical context of the computerized control station of a plant and the way information tokens are used to represent and steer the production process. The empirical observations suggest that semantic comprehensibility (understanding the meaning of information tokens) and referential attribution (relating information tokens to the production process) describe crucial aspects of current work. At the same time, they suggest that the cognitive complexity of software packages tends to render the issue of semantic comprehension much more insidious than that of reference. They also indicate that under ambiguous conditions complex trade-offs between the two develop in which tangible reference to reality is often sought as a substitute for the lack of understanding of the abstract and complex relations mediated by codes and information tokens.

Whereas these issues may be thought of as limited to the contemporary workplace increasingly populated by all sorts of information package, they are also indeed indicative of the broader context of the Internet and the way it is involved in mediating object and social relations. In some simple yet fundamental way the Internet has become a comprehensive and often opaque medium through which the world is perceived predominantly on the basis of data and information tokens packaged in a variety of formats and breeds. In Chapter 8, 'Information Tokens and Reality: A Parable of the Internet', I shift my focus to some of the issues raised by the making of data and information tokens to key cognitive currencies in the wider setting of community and social life. This chapter is a summary of the entire volume and, at the same time, an allegory of the issues the Internet now raises and will continue to raise even more in the future. I pursue this objective by means of slightly unorthodox recourse to fiction analysis. I use and interpret a minute part of Italo Calvino's majestic narrative, *Invisible Cities*, which I suggest can be read as an allegory of the

Internet (much ahead of its diffusion) and the perplexing relationship to reality and agency the Internet mediates.[8] This may be comprehended more easily if the Internet is seen not simply as a huge interlinked system of computing machines made possible by standards and communication protocols but as a prime example of the basic motif of accessing and mediating reality through symbol tokens that forms a key theme of this book. This is one way of reintroducing considerations of time and history into the development of technology in general and the Internet in particular. In this respect, the chapter could be seen as an attempt to present and analyse the perplexing cognitive and communicative issues involved in the historical transition from situated forms of action and communication, embedded in experiential knowledge, to abstract and disembodied systems of representation and meaning construction.

---

[8]The book was originally published in Italy in 1969.

2
The Regulative Regime
of Technology

Introduction

A widespread belief across the social sciences construes the influence technology has on institutions and organizations as being heavily contingent on the characteristics of the social practices with which it gets entangled and the specific make-up of the contexts within which such entanglement occurs. Wittingly or unwittingly, this position is premised on a strong contrast between technologies, on the one hand, and the fabric of local practices and conditions in which technologies are embedded, on the other. The dominant picture is one where technology yields to the human skill or the capacity to bend reality. The forms, accordingly, whereby technological artefacts become involved in local contexts do not depend, at least not predominantly, on the properties of these artefacts. They emerge rather during the process of local implementation, as the functionalities of technologies are negotiated, shaped, bypassed or undermined *in situ*.[1]

Reasonable as it may seem, over the past two decades this assumption has acquired the character of a tacit and unquestioned belief that glosses over significant questions and impedes theorizing on technology and its social involvement. In this context, the fundamental question as to what exactly is the object of *in situ* negotiation has seldom been posited or seriously considered. For, what is negotiated must have an identity of a sort. In its simplest form, negotiation assumes two parties and a problem around which interests or positions are traded-off. It comes therefore as no surprise that limited attention has been given to the obdurate nature of technology and the time-ridden strategies whereby technological

---

[1] See, for example, Grint and Woolgar (1997), Orlikowski (1992, 2000, 2007) Suchman (1996, 2007), Woolgar (2002).

problem-solving and innovation eventually develop and consolidate (Arthur, 2009; Pollock & Williams, 2009). Technologies may not impose unambiguous courses of action, nevertheless, they matter. They make some things easier to accomplish and render others difficult or impossible. Over time, they follow path-dependent trajectories and encase social practices in particular ways of doing things. Given the multivalent involvement of technology in social and economic life, I find it regrettable that social enquiry lacks a vocabulary and a conceptual strategy for describing technologies and artefacts in systematic ways that permit comparisons across contexts and over time (see, e.g., Perrow, 1967).

The focus on technology as object of social enquiry by no means implies a drift away from human concerns and the social practices to which technology is tied. Contrary perhaps to what is often believed, conceiving technologies in generic terms reflects a profound social concern for a fuller appreciation of what is gained or lost as technologies become involved in human affairs. New habits and conventions are established, occupational skills become obsolete or change, goods and services are cheaper, more costly or easier to access, life chances and freedoms emerge or decline as technological artefacts and traditions dissolve one another over time (see, e.g., Borgmann, 1999; Lessig, 2006; Zuboff, 1988). Indeed this is the principal motivation to look beyond the horizon of local contexts. There is no way of appreciating these far-reaching consequences of technological shifts unless one conceives of technology in terms that transcend the limited horizons of local contexts. This chapter deals with some of the challenges raised by the attempt to conceptualize technology in abstract, generic forms that would allow its investigation across contexts and over time, and enable comparison with other coherent forms (formal role systems, normative orders) of governing social practices.

The chapter is structured as follows: The next section discusses some of the limitations consequent upon the disproportionate space given to local conditions in attempting to understand the impact of technology on organizations and social practice. I provide some reasons and examples as to why such an over-reliance cannot address the key question relating to the forms through which technologies participate in the construction of the local by virtue of being negotiated *in situ*. I subsequently state the case for the need to conceive technology as a generic form of regulation that cuts across contexts. In so doing, I outline the distinctive character of technological regulation. This I identify with the strategies of functional simplification and functional closure and the modality of automation. Next, I contrast technological regulation with the two principal regulative regimes of social practice, that is, social structure (formal role systems and hierarchy) and culture (normative regulation). I also identify the distinctive configuration of modalities whereby all three operate. The chapter ends with a reflection on current technological developments (information growth, the Internet) and their implications in terms of regulation.

Artefacts, systems and contexts

The disregard of technology as a primary constituent through which social relations are articulated reflects a miscellaneous array of reasons and motives, more or less justified, as the case may be. Fundamentally, there is the regrettable inadequacy of the technical, engineering view of technology and the assumption of the unproblematic insertion of technology into the context of institutional and community life.[2] The quasi-closed character of the artefacts and technologies of the industrial age designed as 'black-boxes' to be opened only by engineers or experts may to some degree justify such a view. Information artefacts, however, convey an aura of plasticity and flexibility, attributes that have been seen as breaking away from the model of blackbox. At the very bottom, information artefacts are sets of logical instructions providing much ampler space for reconfiguring and rewriting them to address specific problems. Even at the machine interface, ordinary users may choose to engage technology by enacting particular features and functionalities. Widespread sentiment exists according to which information artefacts are revocable and editable (Kallinikos, Aaltonen & Marton, 2010).

There are also, however, other reasons that have contributed to the disregard of technology as an important means of structuring and governing social relations. The diffusion of information technologies and artefacts across the social fabric has driven technology away from the closed and heavily regulated circuits of institutions and organizations towards the open texture of community life (Nardi & Kallinikos, 2007, 2010; Zittrain, 2008). Traditionally, the organizational use of technology has been predicated upon the model of concentration, often justified on the basis of economies of scale and calculations of costs and benefits. By way of contrast, information technologies are assumed to favour scalability, dispersion and ultimately adaptation to individual needs. The diffusion of information

---

[2]By this I do not mean the profession of engineering but the assumption of the unproblematic involvement of artefacts in social practice by social scientists and other actors of the social and political system. Politicians and high government functionaries are particularly susceptible to adopting the naïve view of technology as an unproblematic medium of social engineering.

artefacts throughout the social fabric has therefore come to be seen as implying the decline of the logic of concentration (Benkler, 2006; Castells, 2001; Zuboff & Maxmin, 2003). This diffusion has also contributed to the rise of a consumption-attuned frame that has tended to look upon many computer-based devices as consumer goods, thus losing sight of the engulfing information ecologies in which these devices are embedded and whence they derive their utility.[3] These developments have reinforced the belief in the open and negotiable nature of information artefacts and contributed to shifting the focus of attention away from technology to the social contexts in which technology is embedded.

But even the organizational implementation of large-scale information packages that better conform to the model of concentration has come to be perceived as a largely local affair. The introduction of such packages to organizations has turned out as a much more complicated project than was originally imagined. Despite the consumption of considerable resources, large-scale systems such as Enterprise Resource Planning (ERP) have often failed to meet expectations (see, e.g., Ciborra, 2000). The reasons behind the complexity associated with the implementation of large-scale systems in organizations are surely many and some of them could well be heavily contingent on unique factors. Two lessons, however, appear to have emerged from this experience. First, large information systems are much more ambiguous and open than what has commonly been assumed. Design may influence but does not determine the use of technology. Secondly, social practice and the organizational context within which it develops are fairly complex technical and social entities exhibiting considerable recalcitrance and resistance to technologically induced change (e.g., Avgerou, 2002; Orlikowski, 2000, 2007). The local appropriation of technologies is as a rule contingent on a wide range of professional skills, work cultures and practices, which, being the outcome of longstanding learning processes, may be easy to overlook.

Most of these reasons seem to me poignant, yet they tend to lose sight of the transformative power of technology and the complex web of relations in which it is embedded. Information-based systems and devices are certainly more flexible and malleable than industrial artefacts and technologies. But they are also interlinked in ways that penetrate deep down into the social fabric and participate unobtrusively in the construction of the micro-order of social practice by shaping routines, operations and communicative habits

---

[3] The diffusion of theories such as the *Technology Acceptance Model* represents a case in point. See, for example, Bagozzi (2007) for a retrospective and critical review of that model to which he himself has helped to establish.

(Manovich, 2001). By virtue of being thus interlinked, information technologies are seriously constrained by the demands of compatibility and the functional complementarity to other technologies. Technological design may not unambiguously determine use, but it is not devoid of implications either. Indeed it would be reasonable to assume that design and use, possibility and actuality are interrelated in many and complex ways that have to be disentangled conceptually and studied empirically over time.

A key lesson that emerges from the critical reappraisal of the emphasis put on local relations concerns the degree to which core properties of a technological system may condition its very negotiability and local appropriation (Kallinikos, 2002, 2004b, 2004c; Pollock, Wiliams, & D'Adderio, 2007). Interpretive accounts of technology suffer, as a rule, from an over-reliance on the local 'remaking' of technologies. Such an exclusive focus on local details is susceptible to bypassing the time-ridden formation of nucleuses of technological and also institutional constraints that have been carried over to the design of technologies. Some of these constraints may be negotiable in the short or medium term. More often than not, they are the outcome of path-dependent processes and the forms whereby the strategies of objectification artefacts embody have been laid upon one another over time. Pollock and Williams (2009) demonstrate this forcefully with reference to large-scale, enterprise-wide, off-the-shelf information packages whose essential beginnings go back to the middle of the last century.[4]

A case could therefore be made for the fact that technological solutions and the design of artefacts are usually the outcome of considerable time-ridden developments whereby technologies gradually coalesce and consolidate into complex and recalcitrant textures (Arthur, 2009; Hughes, 1987). Its creative nature notwithstanding, the design of artefacts is a complex social activity, a practice conducted within an established web of understandings that are conditioned by a variety of methods, techniques and discourses. Considered over a larger time span, technological development is shaped partly by cumulative collective learning itself occasioned, at least to some degree, by the use of technical artefacts. These observations ultimately demonstrate the impossibility of considering technology and social practice as simply adversaries (Marton, 2009).

Indeed, patterns of use, solidified over long periods of practice and engagement with particular artefacts, become taken for granted and thus drop out of awareness and their contribution to the design of artefacts forgotten or

---

[4]Chapter 4 provides a variety of factors that limit the negotiability and local adaptation of large-scale information packages.

overlooked. Few technologies develop *ex nihilo* and many of them may indeed be claimed to have path-dependent histories of development, partly driven by the lessons the use of technology delivers over time (Arthur, 2009; Hanseth, 2000; Hughes, 1987). It is thus crucial to observe that use, in this enlarged sense, is not just situated accomplishment as it has often been assumed but a complex social and time-evolving pattern that would be better described as a *praxis*. Rather than being the outcome of a deliberate choice that celebrates the operations of a detached subjectivity, use emerges as a historical force that constructs the user (Kallinikos, 2006). Thus understood, the user is not a transcendental being whose predilections dictate how an artefact is used but a historical construction, in the sense of embodying the longstanding lessons of experience and the social expectations that have developed around technology use and design (Flusser, 2000).

The growing awareness of the complex nature of the situated reshaping of technology may form the basis of transcending some of the limitations of interpretivism and a-historical constructivism while, at the same time, accommodating the lessons they have taught us. Indeed, it would seem timely to question the understanding of technology as primarily a situated exercise, without needing to resort to the old simplifications, typical of a naïve technological determinism. The elusive yet crucial issue of *what* becomes locally negotiable and transformable requires readdressing (Hacking, 1999). Are there any core properties that define the identity of particular artefacts and systems or are technologies just a random bundle of characteristics easy to reshuffle at will and negotiate? To which degree are information systems and applications malleable and interpretable? What does limit or render an artefact or technology malleable? More crucially, who interprets and transforms these artefacts? Are technology and social agents exogenous to one another? The answer to these questions necessitates the investigation of the character of particular technologies and the appreciation of the constraints and limits to their malleability and situated remaking. Some of these constraints may be derived from local or organizational contexts whose activities information artefacts are brought to bear upon. Others, however, could be of another nature and ultimately attributable to the technology itself and the institutional history that its development and use embodies (Arthur, 1994, 2009; Hanseth, 2000).

The controversy surrounding the issue of the interpretive flexibility versus the causal status of technology may well seem as an old and tired debate.[5]

---

[5] See, for example, Bijker (2001), Bijker, Hughes & Pinch (1987); Kling (1992), Orlikowski (2000) Winner (1993, 2001), Woolgar (2002) Grint and Woolgar (1992, 1997).

But it is not. It re-emerges forcefully in the timely issues associated with the diffusion of the Internet and the infected (economically and politically) controversy over the regulative power of code, copyright law and the fate of commons (Benkler, 2006; Lessig, 2002, 2006). It is also ubiquitous in the debate concerning the conception of information based-artefacts as information appliances versus generative artefacts (Norman, 1999; Zittrain, 2007, 2008) and the issues surrounding automation and search engines versus the semantic web (Morville, 2005). Indeed, there is no way of avoiding taking stance on the key issue of the ontology of technical artefacts and how they shape social life. I find it therefore crucial to situate the argument of this chapter as clearly as possible within the rather complex conceptual and empirical landscape that the research on the social and organizational impact of information and communication technologies currently represents.

The central idea I develop in this chapter is that technology could be seen as a distinctive regulative regime that considerably shapes the operations of organizations and institutions and governs social practice. As regulative framework, technology entails an *objectified system of processes and forces* that shape tasks and operations both in the direct way of embodying functionalities that engrave particular courses of action and in the rather unobtrusive fashion of shaping perceptions and preferences, forming skills, routines and professional rules. In this respect, regulation should not be understood in negative terms, as something posterior and exterior brought upon to constrain the space of action of a community of users, already alienated from technological use. In the broad way I use the term here, regulation is constitutive of the processes and operations to which it applies. As already indicated, technological regulation spins out the fabric of social practice constructing its micro-order while embedding it in a much more encompassing context of relations.

In the consciousness of most people, regulation is tied to enforcement institutions whereby compliance with laws, rules and prescriptions is monitored. Therefore, the conception of technology as regulatory instance operating on its own may seem objectionable. The ideas I have put forth so far should suggest, however, that the view of regulation that I adopt is broader and transcends regulation understood predominantly in juridical terms (Foucault, 1977; Burchell, Gordon & Miller, 1991). Technology inscribes and constitutes as much as it prescribes. Therefore, the lack of separate enforcement institutions does not necessarily flaw the idea of technological regulation. This being said, it is worth observing that prescription and enforcement converge in the case of technology and, more specifically, in the case of information-based systems and artefacts. Technological regulation, Grimmelmann notes, is *immediate*: 'Rather than relying on sanctions imposed after the fact to enforce its rules, [software] simply prevents the forbidden behavior from occurring' (Grimmelmann, 2005: 1723).

As I demonstrate in the rest of this chapter, the regulative significance I attribute to technology is closely associated with the distinctive form whereby technology is implicated in human affairs and the shaping of social practices. Technology, I suggest, differs from two other regulative rivals, that is, those of social structure and culture. Social structure (formal role systems, rules) and culture (norms, values, action scripts) have earlier been observed in the literature on organizations and professions and contrasted as regimes of regulation with one another and the institution of the market.[6] Technology, on the other hand, has seldom been seen as more than an arrangement, no matter how complex, of means through which social structure and culture operate. Lessig's pioneering juxtaposition of software *code* with *law*, *markets* and *norms* a decade ago helped, however, to establish the theoretical reasons for viewing technology as a major regulative force and raised the awareness of its regulative implications (see, e.g., Lessig, 1999, 2006).[7] It is therefore extremely important to understand the logic whereby each one of these three basic regulative forces (social structure, culture and technology) operate and appreciate what implications such differences may have for human agency, social practice and institutions.

Technological regulation

Technology becomes involved in social practice in two basic and, in principle, inseparable ways. The first of these appears rather obvious and reflects the *specific functionalities and procedures* embodied in the technological medium. Each technology is a technology of some sort, for example, electronic patient record systems, accounting and finance systems, ERP packages or profiling techniques. Once introduced in a local setting, a technology, by virtue of being a technology of some sort, cannot but come to influence, in one way or another, the *tasks* which it has been called upon

[6]See, for example, Ciborra (1993), Freidson (2001), Ouchi (1979, 1980) and Perrow (1986). I will not deal in this volume with markets as regulative or coordinative regimes. See, for example, Benkler (2006) or Kallinikos (1996).

[7]However implicit this idea is present in Ciborra's juxtaposition of teams (norms), markets and systems (information systems), see his influential book *Teams, Markets and Systems* (Ciborra, 1993).

to monitor and the *social relations* (roles and duties, rules and command structures) clustering around the accomplishment of these tasks. Such influence may well be subject to varying degrees of local reinterpretation and remaking. Yet, it is reasonable to assume that local responses are themselves conditioned by the core functionalities of the technological medium. At the very least, the longstanding involvement of technology in organizations and social practice is associated with the formation and diffusion of skill profiles necessary to operate it.[8]

However, technology is involved in the shaping of human affairs in another less obtrusive and easily overlooked way, namely, as a *generic form for regulating* social and organizational relations. I identify this generic form as developing at the cross-section of two pairs of constitutive principles that I subsume under the terms *functional simplification/closure* and *objectification/automation*. Particular technologies could be seen as specific instantiations (tokens) of the generic form that defines technological involvement in social affairs. This implies that the functionalities a technology embodies carry from the backdoor, as it were, the logic of the constitutive principles of technology. Let me explain.

Contrary to what is often believed, the use of artefacts (information-based or other) is not limited to the enactment of the functionality they embody. It crucially implies trading that functionality against the rich texture of life from which this functionality has originally been abstracted. For instance, speed and precision of information processing often trades off nuance and semantic multiplicity, talk through mobile phones abstract the dense context of communication, car driving engraves a tunnel, as it were, through nature and disregards innumerable landscape details and pleasures. If technologies were merely assemblages of specific functionalities then it would probably have been superfluous to speak of technology in the singular. If the label 'technology' is not merely an illusion created by linguistic convention (and some may claim so) then there ought to be a set of conditions that confer technology its recognizability and difference *vis-à-vis* other important domains of social life. I suggest that it is on the basis of such a minimal yet vital set of requirements (which I make an effort to defend below) that technological artefacts are recognized as different from other means of supporting and structuring human behaviour (Kallinikos, 2006).

The generic form whereby technology is involved in the making of human affairs could accordingly be said to coincide with that minimal set of requirements on the basis of which certain human devices come to be

---

[8]The debates on deskilling, reskilling and e-literacy are indicative in this respect.

recognized as technological rather than as predominantly social or cultural artefacts. Routines and standard operating procedures are, in this respect, social artefacts. By way of contrast, computer software is a technological object. Routines and standard operating procedures may demand techno- logical objects to be executed and technological objects may necessitate routines or standard operating procedures in order to be successfully oper- ated. However, the mutual implication and interpenetration of technologies with social artefacts does not make them similar. That all human artefacts are ultimately social does not save one the task of showing the distinctive facets that make up the mosaic of contemporary social life (Gellner, 1995; Luhmann, 1995). The alternative is indeed to assume an undifferentiated hodgepodge in which everything is deemed social.

Generic forms then, I claim, cut across specific instantiations and dis- close an overall orientation *vis-à-vis* the world. For instance, in his widely acclaimed essay *The Question Concerning Technology*, Heidegger (1977) suggests that modern, science-based technology (as opposed to older pre- modern techniques) regulates human life through *Enframing* (Gestell), which he describes as a distinctive ordering (standing reserve) of the world that technological regulation imposes upon (sets upon) man and nature. Heidegger basically describes the growing of modern technology as an encompassing system, no longer embedded in everyday living (e.g., the windmill) but on the abstractions of science (hydro-electric plant). No matter whether one agrees with Heidegger's highly suggestive yet speculative description of technology, his way of accounting for the distinctive charac- ter of modern technology is indicative of what I would call 'generic forms of technological regulation'. The same holds true for Lewis Mumford's (1934, 1952) account of the different forms of engagement tool versus machines summon, the former being much more open and multi-purpose than the latter.[9] I wish in this chapter to pursue this line of enquiry and juxtapose the way technology is involved in the making of social relations to what I consider as two other major regimes of regulating social practice, that is, formal role systems of which hierarchy is a key model and normative- cultural forms of governance relying on the individual interiorization of norms and action models.

In understanding the significance of technology in these wider terms, Heidegger (1977) tirelessly repeats that 'the essence of technology is not

---

[9]The view of technology as generic form is reencountered in the works of many technology scholars (see, e.g., Arthur, 2009; Borgmann, 1984, 1999; Winner, 1977, 1986).

technological'. This I interpret as meaning that technology as a social form is never exhausted in the functionalities it offers. Given, however, the instrumental context within which most contemporary research is embedded, it comes as no surprise that the detailed study of particular technologies and their specific implications has tended to monopolize the attention of information systems research, organization studies and communication and media research (Kling, 1996).[10] A quick inspection of the key journals in these fields provides strong evidence of this. The same is largely true for research undertaken from a broader social theory-based perspective (Bijker, 2001; Bijker, Hughes & Pinch, 1987). The majority of these studies are studies of some thing. Particular technologies, as opposed to technology in singular, seem just the right avenue for understanding their human and organizational implications even by scholars that have combated narrow interpretivism (Kling, 1996). Could there then be any rationale for dealing with technology in the singular? I suggest so. Particular technologies never exhaust what I call the 'distinctiveness of the technological', in the same perhaps way that a token cannot exhaust the type of which it is an occurrence.

In the end, as I claim in more detail in Chapter 6, the imperative of pursuing research by merely studying particular technologies could be seen as the gradual erosion of all forms of thinking by empiricism (Kallinikos, 2004c). Recognizing the contingent character of most social outcomes does not necessarily preclude theorizing of the type I advocate here. If technology is more than the sum of its applications then the appreciation of its social implications should entail the study of the distinctive and generic forms whereby it is involved in contemporary life (see, e.g., Borgmann, 1984, 1999; Castells, 1996, 2000). After all, an important part of the scientific endeavour should aim at disclosing how generic forms are implicated in particular instantiations and *vice versa* (Cassirer, 1955).

Taking these observations as a point of departure, I consider technology as a generic form of regulating social practice that emerges as distinct against the background of differences it obtains when compared to: (a) formal role systems (i.e., bureaucracies/hierarchies) and (b) rationalized action schemes deriving predominantly from the prevailing cultural models of thinking and doing (Kallinikos, 2004a, 2006). In this sense, regulation through technology could be juxtaposed to the ordering achieved through social structure and

---

[10]This should not, however, be taken to imply that this research is socially useful. It is instrumental in the sense of conforming to a dominant rhetoric and also in the sense of helping researchers publish their research in outlets that further their career advancement.

culture. Generic forms of regulation are analytic or abstract categories and their regulative valence has to be extracted from a bewildering array of cues and situations that make up the concrete and messy world of everyday life.

Following Luhmann (1993), I describe technology as a system or assembly of tasks and operations organized along the lines of *functional simplification* and *functional closure*. These defining technological principles take the form of a set of operations being lifted out of the surrounding institutional and organizational complexity to which they belong, with the purpose of their reconstruction as simplified causal and, in the case of information technologies, procedural sequences, sealed off from their environment.[11] Three major objectives are accomplished that way. *First*, the causal or procedural sequences that make up the circuit of technology represent a considerable reduction of complexity; for, such sequences have been selected out of a much broader range of choices and designed as tight couplings of cause and effects or as strictly ordered procedural sequences. *Secondly*, by sealing off the operations thus instrumented from their environment, it becomes possible to diminish (but perhaps never eliminate) unwanted and uncontrolled interferences from the outside. Closure then represents a means of fencing off contingencies to ensure the recurrent and undisturbed functioning of the operations that constitute the technological system. *Thirdly*, a significant part of the technological operations that are thus simplified and sealed off from surrounding conditions are possible to detach from social contexts and embody their execution in a variety of material devices and objects. As a matter of fact, the embodiment of functions to machines represents an important means for fencing off the system from the contingent responses of humans that may result from doubt, hesitation, negligence or oversight, distraction, forgetfulness and the likes. 'If a then b' is essential to technology.

The essence of functional simplification and closure then coincides with the fact that a series of operations is thus organized as to be considerably cleansed from the ambiguities that may surround their planning and, most crucially, their execution. Thus instrumented, operations become possible to manage, comparatively speaking, in smooth and often efficient ways, by having a considerable part of the carrying out of the operations entrusted into mechanical devices that embody prearranged causal or procedural sequences (in the case of software) in closed circuits. Sealing off and functional closure often implicate the automatic or considerably automated firing of the steps that make up the technological sequence. In the

---

[11]In Chapter 6 I elaborate on how information technology may differ from traditional, materially embodied technologies.

technological realm, functional simplification and closure are thus unavoidable tied to the particular 'animation' of the material, or object universe, by having a significant part of the operations carried out as closed sequences of pre-arranged and automated or considerably automated steps (Mumford, 1952, 1970). Automation, objectification, closure and functional simplification implicate one another.[12]

As already indicated, an essential prerequisite for clearing up targeted operations from ambiguities and transforming them into closed processes coincides with the decoupling or sufficient separation of the technological operations from the institutional and social complexity of the wider system into which these operations are embedded. Ideally, the two systems should be completely separated and their interaction should take place only periodically, under a strict regime of rules that decree who, when and under which conditions are allowed to interfere with technological operations.[13] This applies equally well to operations of nuclear factories, aircraft flight operations, or access to data repositories. When the interaction of the two systems cannot be avoided altogether, then it must so be designed as to take place along controlled pathways (i.e., a strictly regulated interface between the two systems) that do not interfere with the prearranged and automated unfolding of technological sequences.

Under the conditions technological regulation epitomizes, accruing and unforeseeable complexity that may occur, for one reason or another, within the confines of the technological system should be possible to offload and externalize through controlled pathways back to the institutional/ organizational system, which could be able to handle it traditionally, through rules and instructions or by relying on other technologies (Kallinikos, 2005, 2006).[14] Patently, the states described here represent ideal conditions that are only variably met by different technological systems. At the same time, they disclose the entire philosophy of technological regulation and provide a yardstick against which technological sophistication can be measured.

---

[12] I obviously distinguish here between tools and more complex artefacts such as machines in which a series of chained operative sequences are blackboxed. Tools are appended to humans, machines and complex artefacts may not. For more details see Kallinikos (1992) and Mumford (1934, 1952).

[13] Luhmann refers to this interfacing of two different systems and the strict presuppositions by which it takes place as *structural coupling*.

[14] For instance, buses replacing failing trains, road detours failing roads, electricity failing gas supplies, etc. See also Chapter 6 for a more elaborate treatment of this issue.

These observations suggest that functional simplification as a description of the regulative *geist* of technology does not refer to the technological medium *per se*. This last could indeed be very complex in technical or instrumental terms, that is, in its ability to perform particular functions efficiently, as often is the case with many software packages. It rather describes the *relationship* that the technological medium bears to the overall context within which technological operations unfold and to those activities, operations or tasks which it is brought to bear upon. Whereas the operations the technical system embodies represent a substantial simplification, the technical execution of these operations may be carried out in technically complex and eventually efficient ways. The efficiency of technical operations is due partly to the functional simplification of the environment within which they are carried out. Indeed, efficiency often provides the rationale (or the legitimacy) for decoupling a series of operations from the surrounding organizational and institutional complexity and entrusting their execution to technologies.

This suggests that a crucial implication of these design principles is the possibility they provide for magnifying the scale (an aspect of technical efficiency) in which the execution of the tasks and operations that define the technological circuit takes place, for example, an information search through search engines or profiling applications, freeway or railway traffic, nuclear power production, or mass producing technologies. Indeed, the gains in efficiency, often associated with design and implementation of technologies, are the outcome not simply of better opportunities for controlling and monitoring technological operations (Beniger, 1986) but crucially of the possibilities which technological design offers for magnifying the scale on which operations take place (Kallinikos, 2005). The widely used engineering technique of blackboxing (i.e., functionally closing) operations into a technological medium could in this respect be seen as just one expression of a much wider strategy, geared to magnify the scale or intensify the technological operations through functional simplification and automation. In this respect, governance and scale or productivity are inseparable from each other. One can go as far as to claim that efficiency is one particular form of governance rather than a neutral and generic, trans-historic principle.

Regulative regimes

Functional simplification/closure and automation/objectification are the milestones of technological regulation. Taken together, these principles define the ontology of technological systems and artefacts and provide the means for distinguishing regulation through technology from other modes or regimes of structuring and governing institutional practices. Technology proceeds by cleansing its operative domain from ambiguities and by standardizing and streamlining the operations it helps to bring into being, in an analogous perhaps fashion that paving roads is crucial for car driving (Simon, 1969). Ambiguity and recurrent exceptions from the standard ways of coping with a set of tasks defeat the goal of entrusting organizational operations to technology and the pre-specified and standardized responses it implies (Perrow, 1967). Complex and ambiguous tasks can be partly dealt with the aid of technology but that steadily requires *ad hoc* and contingent responses which impede the full realization of the potential of the technological principles described above.

The streamlining of operations brought about by functional simplification and the protective cocoon of functional closure recurs across a wide range of practices that transcend the definition of technology provided here. Classical texts in organization theory construe the development of formal organizations as contingent upon the conception and instrumentation of functionally simplified action patterns, routines and standard operating procedures.[15] Organizations are able to accomplish their objectives through the rationalization (simplification) of jobs and duties and the relative insulation of the environment into which these are carried out from environmental contingencies. Routines and standard operating procedures provide thus the elementary and solid blocks of organizational operations and the social practices that develop within or across organizational boundaries.[16]

It has been a verbal convention to describe such standardized patterns of action as technologies. Rather than being accidental, the naming of routines and standard operating procedures as 'technologies' recognizes the essential similarities which these modes of acting bear to the operations that define technological systems and artefacts (Lindblom, 1981). Both share the simplification of the task environment within which they operate and the relative insulation of that setting from unforeseen contingencies, a condition that allows for the development of recurrent and repetitive patterns. However, to confuse, routines and standard operating procedures and other structured programmes of action with technology amounts to bypassing the essential

---

[15]See March and Simon (1958/1993), Mintzberg (1979, 1983), Simon (1977) and Thompson (1967).
[16]See also Feldman and Pentland (2003), Nelson and Winter (1982), Pentland and Feldman (2005) and Runde et al. (2009).

and defining technological principle of transposing agency to objects by massively offloading the carrying out of tasks from humans to machines.[17]

The reification of function crafted upon objects is fundamental to technology. Without that elaborate objectification that renders specifically developed objects and object processes (software included) able to perform the operations crafted upon them, there is no technology in the modern sense. An important precondition for objectification is the functional simplification and closure of the tasks which technologies will assume. However, to equate the repetitive and strictly structured nature of routines and standard operating procedures with technology on the basis of functional simplification alone amounts to bypassing the critical differences that separate them. Routines and standard operating procedures are critically contingent on human enactment that provides the means whereby rules and stipulations are transformed into actions. For that reason, routines and standard operating procedures are part of job planning and specification and belong to another regulative sphere, that is, the design of duties and the roles by which these duties are associated.

By way of contrast, technologies simplify the process of human enactment by embodying intention and skill to technological processes (objectification). The interpretive process of enactment is limited to the technological interface and even at this level must conform to the premises by which the functionality of machines can be invoked (Kallinikos, Hasselbladh & Marton, 2010). The distinctive ontological and functional profile of technological regulation should thus be distinguished from that of *hierarchy/ formal role systems* that represent another principal mode of regulating social practices to which routines and standard operating procedures belong. Formal role systems occur within the framework of an organizing principle wider than that of functional simplification that, following again Luhmann (1995), I subsume under the label of functional differentiation.

Technological regulation differs too from regulation accomplished through *cultural rationalization*. In contrast to technology and to social structure, cultural rationalization relies heavily on the individual or collective interiorization of norms, the shaping of expectations and the adoption of standard, publicly available, action schemes. As in the other two regimes, cultural

---

[17]It seems to me that the use of the term 'technology' in a wider, associative fashion [e.g., 'technologies of the self' by Foucault (1977)] derives its evocative force by precisely the objectifying principles technology embodies which such associative use invokes to suggest that even soft aspects of human and social life are amenable to strict patterning and regulation. I see that use of the term 'technology' as largely associative and metaphorical rather than literal.

Table 2.1 Regulative regimes and social practice

	Technology	Social structure	Culture
Strategies	Functional simplification, closure	Stratification, functional differentiation	World framing
Modalities	Automation, reification tight coupling	Routines, standard operating procedures loose coupling	Norms, perceptions, expectations loose coupling
Agency forms	Skill profiles	Formal role systems	Models of action, modes of conduct
Objects			**Subjects**

rationalization proceeds by carving out a region of reality upon which it develops the schemes and standards that confer it its distinctive ontology. Norms, expectations and modes of conduct may be specific to particular practices (i.e., medical, legal or accounting, educational or librarian), and the organizational settings in which they are exercised but they may derive as well from the wider institutional system in which these practices are embedded (Friedland & Alford, 1991; Thornton, 2004). These relationships are schematically depicted in Table 2.1 and further qualified in what follows.

Technology could be considered either a functional complement or even an alternative mechanism to regulation accomplished though social structure-building (i.e., social stratification, functional differentiation, hierarchy and role-patterning), or other rationalized action schemes involving culturally embedded action scripts, rules, conventions or policies (Beniger, 1986; Perrow, 1967, 1986). There is a close and historically substantiated relationship between technology, social structure and culture, whereby the one implicates or is driven by the others.[18] Also the development and deployment of technological applications/systems necessitate access to rules and operational regimes and a host of other regulations but these should be distinguished from the very task and procedures embodied on (and thus regulated by) the technological system itself.

The mutual implication of the three major regimes for regulating social practice provides no excuse for failing to recognize the distinctive ontological and operational profile of each of them. There are important insights to be gained by analytically distinguishing technology, social structure

[18]See Introna and Nissenbaum (2000), Mumford (1934, 1952, 1970), Noble (1984, 1985) and Winner (1986).

and culture as generic forms of making and regulating social practices. It is important therefore to further clarify some key similarities and differences. As explained above, social structure presupposes ordering through a variety of strategies that bear strong resemblance to functional simplification and closure (e.g., functional differentiation, routines and standard operating procedures). They too represent a considerable reduction of complexity through careful specification of duties, the standardization of their execution and the stratification of their monitoring and evaluation (see Table 2.1). However, these similarities notwithstanding, formal role systems and procedure instrumentation through rule stipulation can never be sealed off from the institutional and social complexity surrounding them in the way technological systems do. Nor can their execution entrusted, other than in a trivial fashion, to mechanical devises as is the case with cause-and-effect tight coupling, automation and technological reification. Automation is a defining attribute of technological regulation. Functional simplification is crucially undertaken for the purpose of blackboxing and automating the processes or sequences that become thus simplified. In this respect, formal role systems and technology stand as functional alternatives in the manner in which Beniger's (1986) study of the economic origins of information technology suggests.

This last observation restates the basic claim I pursue here that comprehensive *material objectification* and *automation* are essential to technology. These defining attributes distinguish technological regulation from the management of complexity by means of formal role systems. Automation is but a consequence of the distinctive forms whereby technological objectification works. Formal roles systems are generally mapped onto the task segmentation and standardization upon which they bear (Mintzberg, 1979, 1983; Sinha & Van de Ven, 2005) but the two systems remain separate. By way of contrast, technological objectification is both exclusive and expansive. It seeks to translate or replace altogether formal role systems with technological sequences. In so doing, it creates the need for meta-rules of accessing and operating the technological system but this is a different issue. Ultimately, the need for rules that govern formal role systems may never be eliminated but its nature, distribution and degree of involvement substantially change, as technology becomes a pervasive element of social practice. The slim social structure of organizations using high-risk and high-impact technologies is a case in point.

The distinction of technology from norms, rules, conventions and other culturally embedded action scripts may seem easier to make and more straightforward than perhaps the distinction between social structure and technology. In a sense, technology and culture seem at a remove from one another. In yet a different and more general sense, technology is itself a major cultural artefact in the sense of being the product of the particular technical-scientific orientation of the West. In *Technics and Civilization*, Lewis Mumford dedicates the first 60 pages of this monumental work to what he calls the cultural preparation for the technological take-off of Europe (Mumford, 1934). In this respect, technology does embody key cultural orientations that have been, since some time back, the object of substantial debate and controversy.[19]

However, my focus here is narrower and the terms 'culture' and 'cultural rationalization' refer predominantly to instrumental cultures, that is, regions of cultural reality associated with professions and expertise-based social practices. Cultural schemes, norms and rules may well rely on simplification, standardization and often substantial ritualization of behaviour but these means of regulating social relations differ substantially from functional simplification, closure and automation, as described in this chapter. The key difference, as Table 2.1 demonstrates, between cultural and technological regimes of regulation pivots around the emphasis put upon material objectification as a key strategy of control and coordination. No matter the values and predispositions particular technologies may express and the rules they make necessary, they cannot exist as technologies, unless the functions they embody are externalized, materialized and carried out by elaborate and interrelated systems of devices and materially embodied procedures, including lines of code.

Culture, on the other hand, makes extensive use of material artefacts but predominantly as means of expressing cultural predispositions rather than as means of instrumenting cause–effects or procedural sequences. In contrast, technology has an unmistakable outcome orientation (Castoriadis, 1987). It may be used in symbolic ways (gaining legitimacy, signalling modernity) but only by virtue of its pronounced instrumental orientation and the connotations that are or may get tied to such an orientation. In this respect, the major difference between technology and culture as regulative regimes lies in the varying and, to some degree, reverse emphasis put to the objectification versus subjectification processes. Culture constructs subjects in an immediate way. Technology may accomplish such a task only indirectly by means of constructing an object universe that turns upon subjects, aspiring to direct and channel their behaviour by engraving the paths along which subjects can explore their agency (Kallinikos, 2004b).

---

[19]See Arthur (2009), Ellul (1964), Borgmann (1984, 1999), Heidegger (1971, 1977) and Winner (1986).

The differences between the key regimes of regulation identified here are of course subtle and shifting. Most crucially, they presuppose one another and would appear to work successfully under conditions in which each one provides adequate support for the other. For instance, skill profiles and patterns of use (that are associated with particular technologies and are essential to technological regulation) are to some degree modes of interiorizing (through learning) established patterns of action (culture). They also furnish a significant set of criteria (expertise) for designing formal role systems, which are key governance mechanisms for social structure. However, the interpenetration of technological, structural and cultural modes of regulation again provides no excuse for failing to differentiate between them and expose the distinctive logics they exhibit.

Postscript

In this chapter I have sought to develop a framework to account for the distinctive mode by which technology is involved in the instrumentation of tasks and the governance of social relationships centring on the execution of these tasks. I have referred to this mode of task instrumentation and social governance as the 'regulative regime of technology' and juxtaposed it with the modes whereby social structure and culture are involved in the making and regulation of social practice. The implicit reference has always been to the dense and concentrated instrumental and social space of organizations, professions and institutional fields as distinct from society at large. How the alternative regulative regimes of the law, the market and the state may operate within the open space of society has not been considered here.

Little wonder, the ideas presented in this chapter need further elaboration and some of the following chapters pursue that goal.[20] The three-fold distinction of regulative regimes I have presented makes necessary the substantial clarification of those nested territories whereupon technology, social structure and culture encounter one another in ways that make difficult to disentangle and assess (Kallinikos & Hasselbladh, 2009; Lanzara, 2009). There is also a need to spell out more clearly the implications for both

---

[20]The scheme described in Table 2.1 needs to be tested empirically either qualitatively through the intensive study of particular practices and the implications following from the introduction of technologies over longer time scales or quantitatively through cross-sectional research or time series. See Kallinikos, Hasselbladh & Marton (2010) for a further elaboration of the theory and the explorations of its empirical relevance in the context of cultural memory institutions (libraries, archives, museums).

practice and theory regarding what can be learnt by such an abstract and generic treatment of the subject.

Few of the implications appear rather straightforward to me but there may also be others. The first relates to the hypertrophic trends of technological growth, which will inevitably encroach upon judgements and actions derived from the other regulative regimes that are associated with normative orders and formal role systems based on expertise. In vital sectors of the society such as healthcare and justice, architecture, librarianship or finance (and in many others) key decisions will increasingly become entangled in a variety of systems and processes whereby information technologies encode and mediate the realities, tasks and duties that characterize these domains. The outcome of this is the inevitable installation of technological information processes at the heart of activities that were once predominantly performed on the basis of professional criteria (Kallinikos, Hasselbladh & Marton, 2010). This suggests that significant technological developments in particular domains will reflect the allure of functional simplification and superior performance rather than the intrinsic realities of these domains and the expertise systems they have maintained over time (Kallinikos, 2009a; Pollock & Williams, 2009).

For instance, in the case of law, information made available technologically by recording and comparison of accretion, detention and conviction rates may suggest certain criminal acts to have a low rate of conviction on the basis of database analytics of past outcomes (Iannacci, 2010; Schmidt, 2007). The decision as whether to pursue such crimes may therefore be made on the basis of considerations (costs and probability of conviction) that entail a shift on professional codes of practice. Similar and grave ethical issues arise, and will perhaps increasingly do so in the future, from the documentation and information-based management of treatments and category patients in healthcare. In a completely different way, technological developments in data management and the diffusion of computational search (search engines) are currently impinging upon the functioning and the institutional mandates of cultural memory institutions such as library archives and museums. The key services cultural memory institutions provide become gradually indistinguishable from computerized data management and computational search (Kallinikos, Aaltonen & Marton, 2010). These examples suggests that feasibility worked out on the basis of the facilities of computational information processing may impinge upon the institutional mandate of social practices and, in some cases, conflict with professional ethics and what may seem proper or right on the basis of professional codes of practice and institutional principles. While positive social outcomes may be associated with these developments, it is of extreme social relevance to track the consequences of these processes in the long run.

Secondly, there are implications for design in general and the design of information artefacts in particular. The logic of functional simplification works reasonably well within domains that exhibit some stability. The exodus of technology from the closed circuits of institutions and organizations and the diffusion of information artefacts across the social fabric introduce contingencies that artefacts need to deal with (Nardi & Kallinikos, 2007; Nardi & Kow, 2010). Coping with shifting contingencies as opposed to encased and well-defined tasks may demand designing artefacts that are open, interactive and extendible or artefacts that are indeed assembled to specific artefacts by the user on demand (Zittrain, 2008). The designing of artefacts of this sort encounters important trade-offs between openness and performance, current versus future utility. The theoretical ideas presented here provide a framework within which to reflect on these issues.

Finally, the current developments manifested in the increasing significance of information, information infrastructures and the expansion of the Internet disturb the balance established over the past century between the operative independence of technology, social structure and culture and the regulative regimes thus constructed (see, e.g., Kallinikos, 2006). The manner in which information goods, services and processes diffuse across populations challenge the model of concentration and the primacy it has achieved in the production of goods and services. In particular, Benkler's (2006) notion of *social (non-market) production* in which highly valuable goods (e.g., open source software, Wikipedia) are produced in ways that challenge the model of concentration, and the indissoluble ties to property such a model has maintained, may suggest that the key distinctions I make in this chapter need be rethought, modified or expanded. It is my belief, nevertheless, that the appreciation of the far-reaching character of these developments makes necessary the deep understanding of the generic forms through which technology, social structure and culture have been involved in the making and coordination of the social practices that make up the instrumental texture of contemporary societies (see, e.g., Lessig, 1999, 2006). The fuller appreciation of what is currently at stake, what may be lost and gained, necessitates the adequate understanding of technology as regulative regime and the way it both differs and becomes entangled in other regulative regimes in constituting and governing social practice.

3
Bounds and Freedoms: Re-Opening the Blackbox of Technology

Design versus use

Observations of everyday encounters with information systems or technologies suggest that humans frequently use them in ways not envisaged by their designers or developers. Use, as the saying goes, cannot be arrested by design. No matter what or how designers embody functions in artefacts, the context of life is such that new uses emerge out of the habitual deployment of artefacts (Kaptelinin & Nardi, 2006; Orlikowski, 2000). I believe this statement to be correct in principle. However, some of the conclusions that are supposed to derive from this are not, because this state of affairs has frequently been interpreted as ample evidence of the malleable and locally negotiable character of technology. This assumption is neither warranted nor can it unproblematically be derived from the fact that the use of artefacts often confers on them properties other than or additional to those that design embodies. Let me explain.

Conspicuous as it may seem, the incongruity of embodied intentionality and actual use may be difficult to establish empirically. Most technologies are the outcome of several time-ridden developments driven by technical innovation and scientific advance. They also embody the lessons of experience in a variety of contexts in which an artefact may have been used. Such a state of affairs suggests that attributing a legible set of intentions to artefacts may be far more elusive than it may seem at first glance. In technologies with substantial historical involvement in human affairs, the intentions of numerous and successive designers and developers mingle in ways that make the isolation and attribution of a single group of intentions difficult, if not impossible (Arthur, 2009; Hughes, 1987). With reference to whose intentions is the malleability of technology then to be assessed?

Official statements and taken-for-granted beliefs as to what the function of a technology is or how technology works may not provide a proper or, in any case, a meaningful point of departure.

The attribution of a singular intentionality to particular artefacts may, of course, seem reasonable or even straightforward. After all, technologies and artefacts have been produced and used with a specific purpose in mind (e.g., a car is for driving, a knife for cutting, a camera for photographing). And yet such a view considerably simplifies the complex and diachronic texture of functionalities embodied in particular artefacts. This view also attributes an omniscient and too powerful an identity to designers. Usually, the designers of a particular artefact or technology themselves operate within the context of a wider system (design discourse, profession, competition) that significantly shapes their contribution. Such a system is not shaped or controlled by any single agent and it is, above all, not univocal. It grows out of the choices and commitments of many agents employing diverse materials and resources and pursuing concordant or competing strategies across different settings and times. These complexities make the posterior, clear-cut correspondence between intention and artefact use drawn out by an independent observer a rather heroic project.

Take, for instance, a widespread technology such as computer typing that many of us use daily. Word-processing now represents the cumulative development of approximately 30 years of smaller or larger innovations that have improved both the functionality of the software and enlarged the scope of that technology. Word-processing has in addition been influenced by wider developments in hardware and software technology that have impinged considerably on its functionality and leverage. Out of this dense texture, it is impossible to isolate particular intentions, even though the technology is obviously used for writing verbal texts of many kinds. The attribution of a singular intentionality approaches the limit of absurdity when word-processing is placed in the background of the social practice of writing and its uneven path through the ages (Bolter, 1991; McArthur, 1986; Ong, 1982). Word-processing inevitably transcribes and embodies some of the practices and techniques of handwriting, mechanical writing and printing. Out of this complex and historically constituted practice that is computer-based word-processing, one can certainly isolate specific zones of intentions and designs but the technology as such can never be reduced to a single group of intentions. Computer writing, as most technologies, is too broad a category to be directly connected to behaviour. As with every technology, it provides a *standing set of possibilities* (Searle, 1995) that are realized differently each time. In my view, these reasons provide sufficient justification for claiming that the functions technology fulfils in the various contexts of social and institutional life cannot properly be assessed by a putative incongruence between design and actual use.

From this viewpoint, each particular technology emerges as a spectrum of possibilities that have accrued in a complex and diachronic pattern of development that defies description in terms of singular intentions. Whereas major inventions imply breakthroughs, prior commitments and choices often prefigure developments of a particular technology at a given moment. As claimed in the preceding chapters, technologies often evolve in path-dependent patterns that entail incremental improvements geared to accommodate technological compatibility and interoperability (Arthur, 1994, 2009; Hughes, 1987). Isolated intentions projected by an observer onto the technology can never become the arbiter of technological malleability. They can never exhaust the spectrum of embodied intentions that characterize a particular technology nor predict which zone of the population of embodied intentions the user is going to enact.

These observations suggest that technology is involved in human affairs in ways substantially different to what the contrast between design and use by implication asserts. Technology does not influence human agency by imposing a single and mechanical functionality (a 'straw man' argument), as it may easily be assumed. It rather circumscribes a field of possibilities whose realization calls for the active participation of human agents. Rather than imposing single and unambiguous courses of action technology *invites a range of courses of action*. These last are engraved by the distinctive way whereby each technology frames its reference domain (e.g., writing, driving, decision-making) and organizes its basic functions. They are also shaped by the learning histories of each particular technology and the complex texture of intentions and functionalities it embodies. The range of tasks (the leverage) that could be accomplished by using a particular technology is certainly a significant aspect of it. However, the degree whereby humans use smaller or larger enclaves of the spectrum of possibilities embedded in a particular technology does not represent evidence of the malleability and interpretability of technology (Cadili & Whitley, 2005; Orlikowski, 2000). At best it shows user preferences and capabilities. The influence a technology has upon human agency is not reflected in the (non)exhaustive use people may make of the possibilities it offers. It is rather captured, as the preceding chapter suggests, by the distinctive ways whereby a technology invites people to frame a delimited domain of tasks or activities and organize their execution.

The architecture of cognition-based artefacts

These observations suggest that the contrast between design and use does not provide an adequate test of the negotiability or obduracy of technological artefacts. Both use and design are part and parcel of a wider institutional web of relations in which a particular technology finds itself embedded. It is important to remember that each technology is associated with a social practice and the technical and administrative problems confronting it. Patient electronic records, for instance, are associated with healthcare and address the problem of keeping adequate, ordered and easily accessible patient records. Case management systems have been used in justice or other public institutions that deal with individual data histories. Enterprise systems manage the functional interfaces of organizations and provide a unified data space for carrying out, recording and managing transactions. These technologies, as most technologies, develop at the confluence of several technological developments (here computer-based writing, database management, modular architectures, object programming) and practice-related concerns.

Thus conceived, each technology (and the functions it embodies) is too broad a category to adequately frame the issue of technological malleability. Therefore, causal attributions can scarcely be made at the level of technology as a functional whole. Assessing the conformity or incongruence between design and use would demand descending down to minute and unambiguous functions of technology and relating it to behavioural items, a task which experimental psychologists and students of human-computer interaction may find rewarding. And yet, much the same way as the artificiality of experiment reduces the validity of whatever results are thus obtained, concentrating on minute behavioural and technological issues reduces the relevance of the resulting observations as regards the wider issues of how technology as an ensemble of functions, resources and operations relates to social practice and human agency. (I return to this issue later in this chapter.)

There is more to it. The participants, institutions and practices associated with a particular technology form a complex and generative matrix that cannot be tracked down by following the paths and tweaks of intention (and design). Designers and developers, vendors, suppliers, consultants and users mingle together within the framework of institutions and social practices (i.e., markets, laboratories, organizations and regulative bodies) in complex and historically embedded patterns (Hughes, 1987). Consolidated systems of this sort tend to exert an influence on local contexts that is scarcely negotiable in short term (Pollock & Williams, 2009). They frame reality, define options of courses of action, reasonable strategies and methods of evaluating outcomes.

These comments are indicative of the complexity and the analytic difficulties which what may be perceived as the straightforward issue of the malleability of technological artefacts confronts. It is not and, has seldom been, exactly clear as to which aspects of technology are related to which behaviours (uses) and, crucially, how the attributions, if any, are made.[1] Despite insightful research in the field, the issue has as a rule been approached with opaque conceptual lenses that have not been able to penetrate deeply enough the dense texture of relations which they seek to discern. Orlikowski (2000, p. 409), after she has made a strong case for the situated enactment and reshaping of technology through everyday practice, remarks as follows:

> [I]t is important to bear in mind that the recurrent use of technology is not infinitely malleable. Saying that use is situated and not confined to predefined options does not mean that it is totally open to any and all possibilities. The physical properties of artifacts ensure that there are always boundary conditions on how we use them. Conceptual artifacts (such as techniques and methodologies expressed in language) are more likely to be associated with a wider range of uses than software-based artifacts, which, in turn, are more likely to be associated with a wider range of uses than hard-wired machines.

The passage recapitulates some of the dilemmas the issues of technological malleability and the situated use of technology confront. Orlikowski feels that situated use is in the end constrained by what she refers to as 'physical properties of technology' and the 'boundary conditions on how we use them'. But how are these 'boundary conditions' encountered and in what manner are they expressed and perceived by situated users and respected, gotten around or overcome? To these questions Orlikowski responds with a broad typology that portrays technologies as having variable closure/openness depending on whether they are conceptual artefacts, programmable artefacts and hard-wired machines. This, in turn, is closely associated with the range of uses each particular technology admits. The cardinal question

[1] See, for example, Cadili and Whitley (2005), Doherty, Coombs & Loan-Clarke (2006), Lanzara (2009, 2010), Orlikowski (1992, 2000), Rose and Jones (2005), Runde et al. (2009).

then becomes one of addressing how the closure of technological artefacts becomes constructed.

Conceptual artefacts, Orlikowski suggests, are usually associated with a wider range of uses than software-based artefacts.[2] The grid of the former is less detailed and tight than that of the latter and leaves accordingly open more and wider corridors of initiatives and interpretation. Since a huge variety of artefacts exist within each one of the two mentioned categories, it would be of importance to articulate the key properties of artefacts of this sort, which I refer to as 'cognition-based', in a language able to capture and reflect their differences. In what follows, I draw heavily on Nelson Goodman's (1976, 1978) work with the view of constructing an analytic framework that, I suggest, has the promise of untangling obduracy versus malleability of technological artefacts and assess the forms by which they summon human agency.

Despite the fact that Goodman's philosophy of cognition and cognitive organization has had a bearing upon some of the issues artificial intelligence confronts (Ekbia, 2008; Haugeland, 1981), Goodman, it should be made clear, addresses the cognitive organization of cultural (art) artefacts in general and does not deal explicitly with technology. His masterpiece 'Languages of Art' is nonetheless centrally concerned with the relationship between perception and expression, the world as it is or as it is perceived to be and the manner in which is depicted or remade in various arts. A key theme of his book is the distinctive constitution of cultural artefacts such as drawings and music scores and the different forms of human involvement they summon. He tracks differences as systematically produced by the cognitive organization of established schemes of notation (the way a music score differs from a drawing or verbal text) and employs them to account for the variable forms of human involvement with the artefacts these schemes of notation produce.

The affinities of cultural forms (music notation, drawing and verbal writing) to information-based artefacts stem from the basic predispositions both embody as objectified cognitive entities that mediate the pursuit of human objectives through notation. Seen from this perspective, generic cultural artefacts such as the music score could be seen as objectified systems of writing whereby a specific domain of the world (e.g., music) is addressed and reconstituted. As such, generic cultural artefacts embody rules and

---

[2]Note that according to the definition of technology given in the preceding chapter, what Orlikowski refers to as conceptual artefacts do not qualify as technology. Methodologies are part of the knowledge used to produce artefacts but it is not technology in the strict sense of the term.

procedures captured in an elaborate notational language that seeks to structure human action and help it navigate successfully among the contingencies, vagaries or difficulties that may afflict it. The affinities between the score in particular and information artefacts are forcefully demonstrated by the paramount principle of unpacking and separating as much as possible *processes* from *outcomes* that both epitomize.

A music score is a memory aid and set of instructions of how to play a piece of music. The outcome (the music) is produced by carefully and meticulously guiding the performance along the many steps (notes) that constitute the music piece. Information systems are not different in this respect, their prosaic character notwithstanding. They entail a set of instructions on how to manipulate data tokens and items (memory aids) and produce outcomes. While using different semiotic means (to be analysed below), both entail stipulated rules and procedures of how to act upon the domain each one targets (Kallinikos, 1996). There are of course notable differences between the two, the most important being the significant number of automated operations the software entails. The score objectifies and specifies the steps to be followed but it does not entail any automation. However, as I have argued in the preceding chapter, such a clear specification of steps goes some way towards reducing complexity and ambiguity. It is not by accident, I think, that software technology has made significant inroads to music and musical composition (Lanzara, 2010; Pinch, 2008).

Let us now turn to the exposition of how the musical notation, verbal writing and pictorial representation that Goodman refers to with the shorthand names of the *score*, the *script* and the *sketch* respectively differ *qua* notational schemes. As opposed to the score and the script, the sketch is not being produced by recourse to standardized tokens. Pictorial representation does not have an 'alphabet' at its disposal nor explicit rules of combining standardized characters. For this reason it is marked by greater zones of ambiguity than the score and the script and it can never be procedurally reproduced in identical fashion, unless copied in its entirety. Seen as a process and an outcome, the sketch lacks the cognitive organization of rule-based combinations of standardized marks underlying the composition of scripts and, even more, musical notation. To deploy another language, pictorial representation is analogue rather than digital. While certainly obeying a number of culturally embedded rules, pictorial representation exhibits a different cognitive architecture in which the process and the outcome, the means and the ends form an indissoluble bundle and cannot be clearly and unambiguously separated from one another. The cultural rules and skills that underlie the practice of pictorial representation do not have the cognitive status (i.e., standardization, explicitness, precision) of rule-based manipulations of standardized tokens.

The lack of standardized marks governed by well-understood and explicit rule-based combinations makes the steps underlying the (re)production of drawings hardly codifiable and therefore transferable across contexts. The agent encounters the task of drawing without explicit and standardized rules that codify the very process of production and reproduction of drawings. An important consequence is the great degrees of freedom involved in the reproduction and interpretation of pictorial representations. On the other hand, the constitution of the sketch as a dense system renders the (re)production of drawings heavily contingent on the capabilities of the agents involved. While the quality of the final outcome can be judged as more or less successful (that is, a more or less good approximation of what it models), the very process whereby it is produced remains vaguely defined. In this respect, the production of drawings becomes a shortcut for all forms of human behaviour marked by ambiguity (Lindblom, 1981).

The differences between the script and the score entail additional complications and are more difficult to convey. We need to make a distinction here between semantic and syntactic organization and the different planes each one refers to. Verbal writing and reproduction obey the rule-based combination of alphabetic tokens only at the syntactic level. At the semantic level, the text is dense and subject to ambiguities produced by the frequent crossing of the semantic space of one term by others and the impossibility of separating ideas in the fashion one can separate 'a' from 'b' (see also Eco, 1976; Kallinikos, 1992, 1996). The text is thus organized semantically so as to make the finite and unambiguous separations of the meanings its terms carry not possible, in the ways alphabetic tokens can be separated from one another. One can use text-based descriptions and other techniques to delimit the semantic terms of the text, as it is often done in many software programs in daily use. However, at the very bottom the issue is not resolvable this way, whereas the solutions it produces exhibit significant rigidities and limitations (Dreyfus, 2001; Ekbia, 2008). One-to-one correspondences between discrete syntactic tokens and disjoint meanings are rare.[3] The

---

[3] See Chapter 8 for a more elaborate treatment of these issues.

semantic constitution of texts is ambiguous in a fundamental and irreducible way.[4] This is why legibility at the syntactic level does not automatically guarantee identical interpretations of verbal texts.

The score, on the other hand, is both syntactically (standardized music marks) and semantically differentiated. Musical marks correspond to distinct sounds, which may be seen as the equivalence of semantics in music. By way of contrast, syntactically separate terms (that is, words as combination of alphabetic marks) can mingle at the semantic level (that is, 'mammals', 'humans' and 'animals'), leading to overlapping zones and unclear boundaries of semantic units and fields. The ambiguity of the script is precisely due to unclear semantic boundaries. In contrast, the music score is disjointly organized at both the semantic and the syntactic level. For that reason, the music score, Goodman (1976) contends, provides the unambiguous test for deciding whether a performance seen as a situated act is an instance of a musical composition or not. It admits only highly structured forms of human participation. A music score can certainly be interpreted and performed differently but always within a range of options that allows the unambiguous identification of the performance it helps produce as an instance of the piece of music the score represents.

Reassessing technological malleability

Goodman's account of the organization of cognition-based artefacts could be used, I suggest, to produce an analytic map on which human involvement with artefacts can be graded in terms of predictability, accountability and, ultimately, retraceability. At the one extreme, the score, by virtue of adequately separating processes from outcomes, becomes the archetype, or the model if you like, of a cognitive scheme whose elaborate nature lays out the steps to be followed to accomplish the stated outcomes. In this regard, the score represents an efficient process trail that guides human performance amidst the many options it confronts and, ultimately, enables to assess whether it conforms to the prescriptions its elaborate nature embodies.[5] At the other extreme, the sketch/drawing remains the exemplary case of an undercoded process where situated performance (and use) is not

---

[4] The generative nature of verbal language and its unlimited capacity to generate sensible statements owes much to the irreducibility of semantics to discrete or disjoint terms. What ultimately turns out as a problem for technology is a source of inexhaustive richness and infinite generativity for language (Eco, 1976, Kallinikos, 1992, 1996, 1998).

[5] It does so by providing the test by which a performance is assigned to the score.

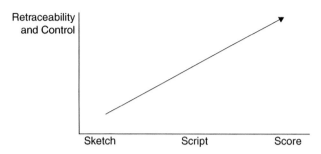

Figure 3.1 Cognition-based artefacts and human behaviour

the instantiation of predefined options but, crucially, the enactment of possible courses of action. These ideas are portrayed schematically in Figure 3.1 below:

Against this backdrop, the far wider range of actions that Orlikowski (2000) attributes to verbal methodologies as compared to software-based artefacts could be traced back and ultimately accounted for by reference to their cognitive organization. Software methodologies formulated in verbal language by necessity contain significant elements of semantic ambiguity. One can work out ways of dealing with ambiguity (including social rules or conventions of interpretation) but as far as one remains within the verbal realm, there is no way to conclusively address or eliminate it. By way of contrast, software-based artefacts exhibit a cognitive organization that essentially recounts the cognitive architecture of the score. Whereas a case can be made for the fact that there is no software without an analysis of the problem that the software is assumed to resolve and which is largely performed and communicated by verbal means (requirements and specification), methodologies and software programs are different kinds of beast. Drawings, on the other hand, represent the exemplary case of human activities that by and large remain outside the regulative jurisdictions of technology. It is possible to work out routines and methods of developing skills for dealing with ambiguity but these can never become objectified to standardized rules and procedures. In the terminology of the preceding chapter, drawing never crosses the distance to the kind of objectification technology entails.

Placed in this context, technology could be seen as that generic social practice by means of which uncertain and ambiguous domains of work and living are progressively untangled, cleansed from ambiguities and brought under its regulative reach. Technology is that transformative grid, the trading zone, as it were, in which ambiguity and contingency are exchanged for certainty and control. Historically, this has taken the form of routine activities taken over by machines (Ekbia, 2008; Simon, 1969). Today, the development of knowledge (i.e., neural networks, fuzzy logic, approximate reasoning) and advances in software engineering (from unstructured to object programming) suggest that significant steps have gradually been made in capturing part of the logic of undercoded modes of action (Voutsina, Kallinikos & Sorensen, 2007).

The amazing variety of software-based artefacts that populate working and living suggests that despite the commonalities underlying their cognitive organization, they still differ in a variety of ways that may be glossed over by the abstract analytic map I propose here. We certainly need ways of capturing the smaller differences underlying software packages in a systematic fashion that allows the fine-grained comparability of software-based artefacts and the disclosure of at least part of the premises on which they rest. How is the transition from the verbal realm to the development of software accomplished? What role requirements engineering plays in this process as an intermediate link? How are differences in architecture (degree of modularity) reflected in the behaviour and functionality of the software and the degree to which it summons human agency? These and other related questions certainly need further consideration.

At the same time, all software-based artefacts are at the bottom numerical and they can accordingly be automated and manipulated algorithmically. The differences in automation notwithstanding, the interaction between humans and machines at the interface could in this case be approached and understood in ways that bear strong affinities to the score and the forms whereby the latter guides human behaviour. It would be possible, for instance, to study how the editing of films and video (numerically-based pictorial representation) through video-editing software (Manovich, 2001, 2010) resembles the account of the score Goodman gives, or whether activities of this sort can meaningfully be approached by drawing on his ideas. It is at the junction of these issues that the contribution of this chapter lies. An important objective I have sought to accomplish has been to unpack the idea of technological malleability with the view of drifting away from a wholesale and indiscriminate analysis of the relevant issues in terms of incongruence between design and use, intention and actual outcomes. Let me, however, admit that the brief exposition of Goodman's ideas on notational schemes cannot do full justice to his rigorous and subtle philosophy; nor can the relevant problematic exhaust the intricate questions which the interaction between human agents and cognition-based artefacts raises. And yet, the ideas I have sought to present in this chapter do capture, no matter how briefly and concisely, the spirit of his work on cognitive architecture and the relevance it carries for understanding the relationship between human action and the artefacts it uses. There is little doubt that much more remains to be done in this direction.

Postscript

The ideas I have presented in this chapter outline some of the operations whereby the construction of micro-orders is accomplished and the interaction between humans and the objects/artefacts they draw on is structured. The malleability of technology is variable and research on how technology and humans interact should seek to transcend the temptation to reason in simple terms that frame the relevant question in terms of either/or. Technological variability can ultimately be tracked to the constitution of cognition-based artefacts, the unpacking of which offers a more nuanced answer as to how human agency and artefacts implicate one another.

At the same time, the design and development of technology takes place within a wider institutional context. The micro-orientation of the issues I have pursued should not be seen as a substitute for the analysis of technology by recourse to analytic means that better address (as in the preceding chapter) the institutional relations in which technology is embedded. Institutions are, however, not disembodied entities. They are themselves sustained by elaborate non-institutional means (Foucault, 1991; Kallinikos & Hasselbladh, 2009). It is not by accident that cognitive closure manifested in the development and deployment of a variety of non-verbal schemes and alpha-numerical systems have historically been major means for constituting action along predictable, recurrent and accountable paths (Beniger, 1986; Cline-Cohen, 1982).

4
Unpacking Information Packages: Rationalization and Governance

Introduction

Large-scale, off-the-shelf information packages have become common-place in organizations over the past two decades. The comprehensive character of these packages certainly marks a distinctive stage in the history of computer-based information technology's involvement in organizations. The need for bringing some sort of uniformity to the disparate ecology of applications and information management techniques that populated organizations was urgent at the time these packages emerged. Interoperability of applications, simple file sharing, computer-based cooperative work and communication across geographical boundaries were and, still are, important to the smooth functioning of contemporary organizations.

Large-scale information packages *prima facie* responded to this need for achieving some sort of integration across functions, departments and task modules. Through these packages organizations have been able to overcome the fragmentation of information sources produced by domain-limited management information systems and construct a relatively unified, organizational-wide software platform. In this regard, Enterprise Resource Planning (ERP) systems, as these packages are usually called, became a computer-based administrative framework for planning, conducting and monitoring a large array of functionally segmented operations in ways that both accommodate in real time the intrinsic cross-functional interdependencies underlying these operations, and enable their posterior retracing and control.

ERP packages do not, however, mirror a pre-existing organizational world. Rather, they are both a pervasive and potent means for restructuring organizations and represent a good illustration of the claims advanced in Chapter 2 regarding the regulative implications of technologies. ERP systems establish distinctions and work items throughout the organization, connect them within and across functions, bring about standardization in input and output data and set up elaborate procedures to be followed with respect to the execution and monitoring of organizational tasks. In this and the next chapter I lay open a set of implicit yet crucial organizational and behavioural premises on which large-scale information packages such as ERP systems have been built. More specifically, I focus on the impact ERP packages may have on mediating a conception of organizations as just *assemblies of functions* and processes and of human agency as no more than the *enactment of routines and procedures* possible to embed on software. These are strong predilections with far-reaching implications within and across workplaces that have by and large escaped the relevant literatures.

ERP packages can certainly be studied and ultimately evaluated in terms of performance and as instruments for promoting efficiency. However, the extent of their involvement in organization carries important implications that reach deep down to the instrumentation of everyday duties and tasks. In providing information within and across functions, organization-wide information packages become important means for governing organizational operations and evaluating outcomes. A distinctive characteristic of information systems of this sort is the reconstruction of the very microecology of organizational operations to which any single transaction belongs. By transactions, I mean information transactions as these are exemplified by the recording, processing and transfer of information associated with the planning and execution of the minute and routine tasks (and their subcategories) that make up the daily texture of organizational life.

In the world ERP systems help bring about there are no isolated tasks. Most organizational transactions impinge upon others and their effects must thus be recorded and accounted for. Transactional interdependencies are thus carefully defined or recorded and their execution becomes accordingly codified. By recording and interlinking organizational transactions, ERP packages provide the transactional infrastructure and the cognitive means that sharpen the awareness of the effects which one's actions may have on others and indirectly on oneself. ERP packages therefore bring the dream of a wide organizational transparency/visibility a step further towards its technological perfection. Any organizational change, from the most minute (e.g., goods movement in the warehouse) to the most encompassing (e.g., production rescheduling), is recorded and its organizational impact on other functions or states captured through interface connections to other modules or sub-modules (Fleck, 1994). In so doing, ERP packages inexorably shape human agency at work by constructing workflows that proactively stipulate and bundle together the steps that have to be followed in order for a transaction or series of transactions to be accomplished.

For instance, vendor evaluation in the SAP/R3 *Materials Management* module comprises the following criteria for evaluating suppliers: price, quality, delivery, general service and external service (Bancroft, Seip & Sprengel, 1996).[1] The information about the suppliers recorded in the database is structured along these dimensions and, in addition, the system provides information about past performance of suppliers. This way the system stipulates the steps necessary for the evaluation of suppliers (a subtask within the wider task of choosing and placing an order) to take place. At the same time, the links of placing an order to *Financial Accounting* and *Controlling* modules and the *Warehouse Management* sub-module help establish the awareness of the effects one's choices may have on others and the organization (Bancroft Seip & Sprengel, 1996; Ptak & Schragenheim, 2000; Soh, Kien & Tay-Yap, 2000). It is in this respect that organizational-wide information systems move a step further in shaping human agency in organizations than specialized information systems or stand-alone artefacts.

Aligned with the analytical predisposition of the entire volume, ERP packages are here treated as independent products capable of being analysed in their own right, without reference to the contextual dynamics whereby they are often reshaped and their functionality reconfigured. This is not an uncontroversial stance (see, e.g., Fleck, 1994; Wagner, Scott & Galliers, 2006) but one that is driven by the wider concerns I developed in Chapter 2. Let me therefore restate that analysing ERP packages in these terms does not of necessity discard or downplay the significance which the implementation process may have in reshaping these packages to the demands of particular organizations. Implementation, as Fleck's (1994) seminal article has successfully demonstrated, is not a procedure of unproblematic installation but rather a complex socio-technical process of renegotiation and redevelopment among various stakeholders (see also Quattrone & Hopper, 2006).

However, no matter how important, the changes brought about during the implementation phase do not exhaust the effects ERP packages have

---

[1]Subsequent releases of SAP/R3 have enriched one or other detail of the steps and operations embedded in modules and crucially 'brought the package' to the Web but left its logic intact.

on particular settings. Many of these modifications are performed on an anterior system of solutions mediated by the ERP package. Local adaptation becomes by necessity framed and heavily conditioned by the overall philosophy and structure (data items and fields, procedures, cross-functional processes) onto which the package is predicated. It is also influenced by the solidified nature of the solutions any package of this sort embodies that are the outcome of the trajectory of ERP technology through time.

Drawing on these ideas, I argue that the analysis of large-scale, integrative information packages irrespective of their implementation is justifiable on several counts. First, contextual adaptation and reshaping of such packages cannot undo the logic and the very presuppositions on which the package is predicated. For instance, other criteria may be added by particular organizations to those referred to above in connection with vendor evaluation. But the evaluation is still made and justified by recourse to a number of discrete criteria, and the information that the system is capable of providing. Other forms of evaluation based, say, on loyalty or opportunism, holistic or tacit information not possible to supply through the system are thus forgone or become subordinated to the logic the system embodies (Fleck, 1994). Secondly, contextual adaptation is conditioned by characteristics of technology that become blackboxed and thus escape or withstand deliberate manipulation. ERP packages in particular are solidified technologies whose complexity usually transcends the ability of particular groups or organizations to rework the code, reprogramme or redefine the logic on which any such package is based. Thirdly, the adequate understanding of the issues occasioned by any technology, not merely ERP systems, entails the depiction of common elements that cut across specific cases. To these factors one should add the complex institutional and economic relations whereby ERP packages are sustained) and which are hardly negotiable *in situ* (Hanseth, 2000; Pollock & Williams, 2009; Sawyer & Southwick, 2002).

Reflecting these preoccupations, this chapter approaches and analyses ERP packages independently of the ways whereby they may be contextually reshaped during the process of implementation. The ultimate purpose is to attempt to disclose the logic or action 'philosophy' onto which these systems are predicated, and to lay open the forms of human agency, organization and work which they appear to implicate. Prior to this, however, a brief review of current research on ERP and information infrastructures is undertaken. The review suggests that the critical examination of the organizational and behavioural foundations of large-scale information systems to remain by and large an uncharted territory.

Current research on off-the-shelf information packages

The literature on ERP Packages is fairly heterogeneous and comprises several strands of thought and practice.

To begin with, a technical or quasi-technical literature with strong managerial focus has sought to provide the guidelines for the successful implementation of information platforms as those exemplified by ERP packages. The major concern of this literature has been the development of methodologies, tools and techniques necessary to accomplish this goal (e.g., Bancroft, Seip & Sprengel, 1996; O'Leary, 2000; Ptak & Schragenheim, 2000). While being primarily concerned with practical issues relating to the implementation of ERP packages, this narrowly prescriptive literature cannot avoid addressing the working practices, operating procedures and the human skills necessary to successfully deploy this technology. After all, the implementation of ERP packages demands the 're-engineering' of the organization. This of necessity implies new methods for designing tasks, jobs and work modules and leads to new work structures and procedures. However, these issues are most commonly framed in strictly technical terms. Despite the inevitable focus on issues of work, the behavioural assumptions underlying the implementation of ERP systems are never examined in this rather technical literature. The definition of tasks and their bundling to larger sequences or processes, the construction of roles centred around these processes, and the constitution of human agency along distinct lines that may reflect the meticulous segmentation of work and the overall architecture of packages are not given particular attention (e.g., Markus et al., 2000).

A different research agenda with a blend of descriptive and prescriptive goals has been documenting various problems and issues relating to the introduction of ERP packages in organizations. Attention has been given to a range of factors thought to influence the successful implementation of ERP packages, for example, the size of the package and the number of users concerned (Francalanci, 2001; Kumar, Maheshwari & Kumar, 2003; Markus et al., 2000), the pattern of implementation activities and its temporal effects (Sawyer & Southwick, 2002), the significance of organizational and national cultures (Krumbholz et al., 2000; Soh, Kien & Tay-Yap, 2000) and learning (Fleck, 1994; Parr & Schanks, 2000), and the patterns of knowledge transfer from the supplier to the host organization (Lee & Lee, 2000; Parr & Schanks, 2000). Some studies have investigated the significance of the designing methodologies, as these are reflected in the overall architecture of the package and the flexibility this last provides for rapid environmental adaptation (Fan, Stallaert & Whinston, 2000; Sprott, 2000). Other studies have investigated the way best practice is embedded on the software (Markus, Tanis & Van Fenema, 2000; Wagner, Scott and Galliers, 2006).

Many of these studies contain occasional comments on the effects of long-driven standardization brought about by ERP technology and the restructuring of organizational tasks along the lines suggested by 're-engineering' (see, e.g., Kumar & Van Hillegersberg, 2000). Several studies have focused on specific behavioural aspects, that is, the relationship between national and organizational culture and ERP implementation and use (Krumbholz et al., 2000; Soh, Kien & Tay-Yap, 2000), the temporal effects on work and organizational patterns associated with ERP implementation (Sawyer & Southwick, 2002) or the influence ERP systems have on organizational structures and processes (Markus, Tanis & Van Fenema, 2000; Soh, Kien & Tay-Yap, 2000).

It is impossible to do justice to such a wide and heterogeneous literature. But it would not be unfair to say that the overwhelming majority of the studies in these two strands of literature reviewed here are, in the end, marked by a strong prescriptive orientation.[2] The majority of these are studies of the factors that may inhibit or facilitate the successful implementation of ERP systems. At the very bottom, they are concerned with developing guidelines for selecting, implementing successfully and managing such systems. Wider issues relating to the nature of work and its transformations as well as the structural templates whereby work has been historically accommodated and that ERP systems impinge upon have been bypassed or ignored by these rather prescriptive literatures.

A different set of preoccupations is reflected in the work of Ciborra and his associates.[3] Drawing on a limited number of intensive case studies, Ciborra and his associates have showed large information packages or 'corporate information infrastructures', as they call them, to be only partly subject to deliberate manipulation and planning. A complex tangle of technological interdependencies (some technologies or components fit only with certain others) combines with the needs for standards across various component technologies to limit discretion and the space of choice. Furthermore, the technological, organizational and social embeddedness of the various components of technology (each component is embedded in a complex network of other technologies, commercial interests and social practices external

---

[2] Of those I have referred to here notable exceptions are Fleck (1994), Quattrone and Hopper (2006), Sawyer and Southwick (2002), Wagner, Scott & Galliers (2006).
[3] See, for example, Ciborra (2000), Ciborra and Hanseth (1998) and Hanseth and Ciborra (2007).

to the organization) join the previously mentioned constraints to make large-scale, off-the-shelf information packages a recalcitrant ally. Taken together, all these factors tend to produce complex socio-technical assemblages that evade control and undermine the very reasons (the quest for control) for which they were implemented. Not infrequently, solutions of problems in one domain export them in other domains or, crucially, recreate them at an even more comprehensive level. Often, the accumulation of side effects drifts the implementation of large-scale information packages along directions that were never imagined at the very moment of their inception into organizations. Integration is thus subject to double-bind effects. It both enables and undermines control and purposeful action. Similar observations have been delivered by Fleck (1994) in one of the earliest implementation studies of large-scale information packages.

A distinctive position in all this literature occupies the work of Pollock and Williams and their attempt to understand ERP packages in broader terms that recount both the governing nature of this technology and its long developmental trajectory (Pollock & Williams, 2009). A key motif in their work concerns the processes whereby off-the-shelf information packages inescapably become generic solutions, sold to an impersonal market (see also Pollock, Williams & Procter, 2003). Labelled as the *generification* thesis, this argument describes the logic and the processes whereby ERP packages need to abstract from particular details to become an adequately abstract and generic template of information-based transactions and operations possible to sell to a variety of organizations (small or big, public or private) across the globe (see also Pollock, Williams & D'Adderio, 2007). In thus becoming generic solutions, ERP packages need to be recontextualized to respond to the specific nature of tasks and modes of operating, underlying particular organizations. But such a recontextualization (implementation) cannot be an innocent adaptation to the realities of the adapting organization but rather a complex process in which implementation is significantly framed by the logic and the structure of the generic solution. What can thus be adapted to local conditions is prefigured by the package, which in some way becomes a straightjacket. The ideas I pursue in the rest of this chapter show some of the perplexing and subtle issues engendered by the recontextualization of generic solutions.

Let it be clear that the studies reviewed here represent but a small sample of a very large literature that has been occasioned by the growing organizational involvement of large-scale integrative packages.[4] However, its

---

[4]See Moon (2007) for a systematic review of the literature entailing 313 journal articles.

limitations in terms of representativeness notwithstanding, the review is, in my view, indicative of the very questions that have received overwhelming attention so far. The majority of studies on large-scale, off-the-shelf information packages have been studies of implementation and the problems this engenders. A considerable portion of these studies has had a pronounced prescriptive orientation concerned with the successful implementation of ERP packages and its contribution to raising the performance of organizations into which they are introduced. A smaller number of other studies have explored wider issues concerning how work and organizational adaptation occurs locally despite the heavy focus on package implementation. With few exceptions (e.g., Ciborra, 2000; Pollock & Williams, 2009) these traditions overlook the wider implications of technology and its regulative *geist*, as described in Chapter 2.

On the basis of a broader historical evaluation of technology and the concerns laid out in Chapter 2, it would be possible to conjecture that the organizational involvement of integrative packages accomplishes much more than improving the performance of organizational operations. It too reconfigures the design and execution of organizational tasks, shapes the work environment of employees, and impinges upon their behaviour (Kling, 1996; Zuboff, 1988). As already suggested, large-scale technologies of integration segment organizational tasks in specific ways, they combine them into sequences and workflows, often extended across functions and task modules. They do so in terms that cannot help but reflect a number of assumptions concerning what an organization is and how work is structured and carried out in organizations. Brought into particular settings, the hidden premises of ERP packages inevitably shape the processes and structural templates of organizations as well as the forms whereby human agents come to relate to the object of their work and to one another. Let us now examine these issues.

The hidden organizational premises of ERP systems

ERP packages straightforwardly address issues of organizational integration across functions and locations. Organized in function modules that draw on a common database, an ERP package establishes inter-modular connections that recapture the cross-functional interdependencies of organizational operations. At the same time, the modular architecture of the package allows for functional autonomy and flexibility that address the specific requirements of each functional module. Gauged in sheer technical terms of information-processing, the overall architecture of ERP systems introduces significant innovations. However, placed in the wider context of the variety of organizational practices and the structural blueprints that have been known to accommodate organizations, ERP technology definitely appears less innovative.[5] Let me explain.

The organizational blueprint onto which ERP technology is predicated seems to recount a rather traditional understanding of organizations. Indeed, organizations are conceived as systems comprising major groups of activity that, by and large, coincide with the conventional functional segmentation of organizations, that is, production, marketing, product development, purchasing and warehousing, human resource management, finance and accounting (see, e.g., Mintzberg, 1979; Wigand, Picot and Reichwald, 1997). Major operational modules in ERP packages available in the market today are based on this functional understanding of organizations. This rather traditional way of conceiving organizations is considerably reinforced by the establishment of more narrowly defined categories that break functions down into sub-functional domains. For instance, the SAP/R3 *Human Resource* module establishes sub-functional categories such as 'pay roll, benefits administration, applicant data administration, personnel development planning, workforce planning, schedule and shift planning, time management, and travel-expense accounting' (Bancroft, Seip & Sprengel, 1996, p. 33). Organizational functions and sub-functions are crucial building blocks of ERP packages.

However, in providing the means for connecting operations across functions, ERP technology is claimed to transcend the conventional function-based organizational template. The successful integration of the temporal, functional and structural differentiation of organizational operations presupposes the restructuring of organizational operations along the lines suggested by 're-engineering' (Bancroft, Seip & Sprengel, 1996; O'Leary, 2000). 'Re-engineering' is known to demand the establishment of cross-functional processes in ways that provide a clear orientation towards the market, or any other crucial external referent of the organization. The many discrete steps that make up the production of goods and services (i.e., functions and sub-functions) must thus be defined and tied together so as to construct the trail (the business process) towards the ultimate or intermediate destinations, that is, the customer of the organization or other units of the same organization, as smooth as possible. A process view of organization, assumed to provide the means for

[5] See, for example, Ciborra (1996), Hedlund (1986), Mintzberg (1979) and Nonaka (1994).

responding to the demands of the market or other internal constituents, is thus juxtaposed to the conventional functionally based organizational structure and its admittedly inward orientation.

And yet, at a closer scrutiny, this picture seems to be rather idealized and the claim of external orientation strongly overstated. The identification of functional and cross-functional processes and their system codification must pass through the bottleneck of the technical prerequisites of computer-based engineering of solutions and the state of the art of the technology at the time of implementation. The way to the market is neither straightforward nor without binding presuppositions. ERP technology, as perhaps any technology, reconstitutes organizational operations only after it has broken these operations down into long-driven detail. The meticulous definition of data items, the precise identification of transactional steps, and the fashioning of such steps into clearly described sequences that cover the operations of the entire organization are essential to the computer engineering of ERP packages. Out of this far-going fragmentation, it becomes increasingly difficult to bundle tasks in sequences that target the external environment of organizations. The huge amount of details in which the completion of the various operations (e.g., warehousing, accounting) is usually immersed obscures the road to the market and increases the risk of these operations being cut from the ultimate destination these packages are claimed to promote (e.g., customer satisfaction).

It is vital to assess the organizational implications of what at first sight may seem evident. ERP systems recount a view of organizations as a huge series of procedural steps, tied together to sequential patterns, subfunctional categories, modules and cross-modular transactions embodied as information-based operations. The unspoken or hidden premise onto which ERP systems are predicated assumes that organizational operations can ultimately be reduced to a large series of procedural steps, irrespective of culture, context and significance these operations may have had. On this account, organizing is no more than the *transactional mechanics* whereby these steps are assembled and coordinated. Beyond this focus, other forms of human involvement at work and organizational practices that are hard to pin down, yet crucial to the ways things are usually done, are ignored and bypassed (Fleck, 1994; Soh, Kien & Tay-Yap, 2000). The syntax of ERP systems merely entails carefully defined data items, transactional steps and rules for assembling them into various combinations. Placed in such a context, the meaning of *process* tends, in fact, to dissolve into that of *procedure*, that is, a linear sequence of discrete transactional steps necessary to accomplish a certain task (Sawyer & Southwick, 2002).

These claims can be exemplified by reference to any of the commercially available ERP packages. The SAP/R3 *Materials Management* module, for instance, divides the totality of operations relevant to the identification, procurement and internal distribution of inputs into the following eight data/action categories: *purchasing, external services management, vendor evaluation, inventory management, invoice verification, warehouse management, consumption-based planning* and *material ledger.* Each of these categories or steps is further broken down into subcategories or steps. Inventory management, for instance, comprises the following data or action subcategories: *material master, data inventory management, goods movement, environment, planning goods receipts, goods receipts for purchased orders, reservations, goods issues, transfer posting* and *stock transfer, print functions* and *physical inventory.* Even these subcategories are broken down into minute data items of steps. For instance, the subcategory 'good issues' identifies the following distinct groups of operations: *deliveries to customers, withdrawal of material for production orders*, other *internal staging of material, return deliveries to vendors, scrapping and sampling* (Bancroft, Seip & Sprengel, 1996).[6]

Now it is well known that the design and engineering of computer-based information systems in general are predicated on the meticulous segmentation of the operations that these systems mediate.[7] Such in-depth segmentation of the domain upon which the system is brought to bear is essential for defining the data items, the steps and the rules whereby they are combined into transactional sequences. ERP systems cannot differ in this respect. The proceduralization then of organizations could be seen as the inevitable outcome of computer-based automation in general rather than the outcome of the distinctive logic underlying ERP systems. True as this may be, ERP systems accentuate some of the problems that seem to be intrinsic to procedural standardization and computer automation. Owing to their comprehensiveness and depth, ERP systems tend to construe nearly the entire scale of organizational operations (rather than particular operations or tasks) as an extensive series of transactional steps. After all, ERP technology aims at mapping organization-wide flows and transactions rather than constructing domain-limited information systems. In this respect, the comprehensive nature of ERP packages carries important structural and workflow implications.

---

[6]The differences subsequent SAP releases introduce do not change this picture. Indeed, in being more detailed in some cases, these newer versions reinforce the validity of the claims I make here.

[7]For example, Brooks (1987), Dreyfus and Dreyfus (1986), Newell and Simon (1981), Simon (1969) or Zuboff (1988).

The conception of organizations in procedural terms compelled by powerful ERP packages is almost certain to have far-reaching implications. That is, the comprehensive pre-structuring of data items and the detailed specification of procedures (i.e., pre-programming of execution patterns) inevitably reduce the space of open, people-to-people encounters. They also impose significant constraints to less structured ways whereby humans may relate to their work and work objects.[8] Ultimately, they construe organizational behaviour in terms of *procedure enactment*. Never before in history of the West have organizations been as standardized and unresponsive to contingencies as they are today, despite assertions to the contrary. What does not conform to the categories, task descriptions and routines which large-scale information packages mediate is prone to fall off the edges of attention and be disregarded.

The procedural standardization of organizations that ERP systems bring about transforms significantly the context within which human effort is exerted. To some degree it purifies traditional work practices through *ex ante* rationalization that cleanses what is deemed irrelevant or impossible to achieve through automation. This streamlining that recounts the project of functional simplification analysed in Chapter 2 occurs against a background of behavioural diversity, in which work behaviour seldom conforms to a linear progression from perception through interpretation to action (Styhre, 2008) entailing testing, sidesteps and improvization (March & Olsen, 1989; Weick, 1979a, 1979b, 1993). These issues are dealt with in greater detail in the next chapter. Before I turn to the examination of these fundamental issues, I need briefly to return to the issue of the external orientation of organizations which the organizational involvement of ERP packages is supposed to facilitate.

Functional prerequisites versus external adaptation

As noted, the meticulous and comprehensive segmentation of organizational operations underlying ERP packages may work at cross-purposes with the goals of customer satisfaction and market adaptation which these packages are said to promote. The reason for this is the huge number of procedural steps that define the system. The conception of organizations in these terms ends up in the detailed segmentation of operations across the organization, a condition that may ultimately impede the strategic purpose of responding

[8]See, for instance, Allen (2005), Fleck (1994), Pollock, Williams & Procter (2003), Sawyer and Southwick (2002).

successfully to the demands of the environment. In the meticulously parsed universe of ERP systems, the ultimate goal of responding to external conditions may be obscured and accordingly get lost in the maze of transactions that reconstruct organizations as extensive procedural fields. Concern with the management of internal processes and the accommodation of the bits and pieces of the various transactional groups and modules may obscure and finally replace external adaptation.

It is often suggested that the problem of external orientation can be overcome by distinguishing core processes from support processes. The managerial literature suggests that in most organizations, core processes, that is, processes that are responsible for the major building blocks of an organization's products or services, range from half to one dozen (Bancroft, Seip & Sprengel, 1996; Ptak & Schragenheim, 2000). Accordingly, it is possible to separate core processes and place them at the centre of organizational operations and annex to them all other activities that are viewed as supportive. After all, this is the essence of *re-engineering* that ERP packages are supposed to promote. It should, however, be made clear that this strategic vision cannot unambiguously be embedded in the software and has to be maintained by human initiatives *vis-à-vis* the routines that mark the execution of daily duties, a task that is notoriously difficult. Faced with the cognitive complexity of the package, ordinary users and managers may lose sight of the wider purpose their contributions are supposed to serve. This is undeniably a perennial organizational problem that predates ERP packages (Chandler, 1977; Mintzberg, 1979) but which is nonetheless accentuated by the analytic reductionism and far-reaching segmentation of organizational operations that these packages bring about.

These claims are better appreciated against the background of widespread habits and behavioural responses human displace under conditions of complexity and ambiguity (March & Olsen, 1976). It is indeed a common response to turn one's back on cognitive complexity, resort to simplified cause-and-effect relations that are concordant with established beliefs and habits and, ultimately, to retreat into one's own limited and seemingly controllable zone of duties.[9] In this sense, the comprehensive character of ERP packages and the cognitive complexity underlying them are prone to reintroduce the very fragmentation and sub-optimization that they have set out to combat (Allen, 2005). It is well known that the loss of the perspective into which particular transactions must be placed is among the principal

---

[9] See, for example, March and Olsen (1976, 1989), Turkle (1995), Weick (1979b, 1993) and Zuboff (1988).

reasons for sub-optimization, and people's concomitant difficulties in perceiving the role they have to play within the greater organizational system (March & Simon, 1958/1993; Mintzberg, 1979).

The internal orientation of information packages has been widely acknowledged and has severely been accentuated by the importance which the Internet has acquired over the past two decades for most organizations. It comes therefore as no surprise that the major developers of packaged software have sought to provide interface solutions that connect these packages to the growing information universe of the Internet, clothed in an appropriate rhetoric of market orientation. But it would be naïve to believe that the internal orientation of ERP packages is an issue of attitude and data transmission standards (the interface).

I do not wish to enter the rather cumbersome theoretical underpinnings of *boundary-making* and how *system formation* inevitably implies the accommodation of internal units and processes and makes internal orientation and self-reference indispensable (see, e.g., Kallinikos, 2006; Luhmann, 1995). Suffice perhaps to restate that the comprehensive character of ERP systems plays an important role in the very internal orientation which software packages of this sort are bound to exhibit. For, the many data items, transactional steps and processes must be fashioned into a working whole. Such a task cannot be accomplished unless the system accommodates its internal relations and dependencies (Kallinikos, 2006). Indeed, the higher the number of components and items in a system, the greater the need to fashion these items and components into a working whole by taking care of internal dependencies and technological compatibilities. These observations suggest that the forces that drive the internal orientation of ERP systems are endemic in any system of that magnitude and cannot be reversed by the rhetoric of best practice and market orientation deployed by ERP vendors and consultants.

Off-the-shelf information packages are basically concerned with dissecting the complex texture of organizing into discrete steps with the ultimate purpose of raising the manageability of organizations. The project of depicting the interdependent character of organizational operations and the way the various tasks and the information they generate bear upon one another is motivated by the desire to render the entire system of internal relations predictable and controllable. Though dressed in the still-fashionable rhetoric of business processes and market adaptation in the age of the Internet, ERP packages are by implication inward looking (Kumar & Van Hillegersberg, 2000), being concerned with tying together the overwhelming part of the internal relations and activities of an organization. The primary goal is less to contribute to the adaptability of the organization to external contingencies than to build a detailed map of the organizational territory that can be used as the springboard for organizational action and the control of the organization. In the last resort, ERP packages aim at raising the manageability/control/predictability of the organizational system's routine operations. This could be a noble goal but one that has to be explicitly acknowledged.

These claims suggest that that the organizational involvement of ERP packages is bound to have implications that derive from the predominantly inward-looking orientation of such packages, and the very organizational premises on which they are predicated. Large-scale, off-the-shelf information packages imply the comprehensive design of items, relations and operations moulded into a management model that could be brought to bear on any organization (Pollock, Williams & Procter, 2003; Soh, Kien & Tay-Yap, 2000). It is obvious that the design of such a system is based on an abstracted, shorthand version, no matter how rich in details, of organizational operations. It therefore represents a decontextualized (i.e., deprived from particular characteristics) accomplishment that can, in the best case, be adjusted *a posteriori* to fit the circumstances of the particular organization, whose tasks the ERP package is called upon to monitor (Fleck, 1994; Koch, 2004).

Now, the vendor/consultant industry built around the commercial exploitation and implementation of ERP packages would claim that a package of this sort cannot be brought to bear on the management of an organization, unless the tasks and processes underlying the host organization are studied in detail. It is only through such a detailed study that the package can be adapted to the specific contingencies facing that organization. The effort and the time spent (several years) for adapting ERP packages to particular organizations suggest that their implementation constitutes a complex venture that cannot be brought into being unless significant portions of the package are negotiated locally.

How genuine such an adaptation to local circumstances may become is an issue that falls outside the scope of this chapter. As has been indicated in the introduction of this chapter and elsewhere in this volume, there is definitely variation on the extent to which implementation processes may reshape such off-the-shelf information packages. However, local adaptation is also subject to powerful constraints (Fleck, 1994; Kallinikos, 2002; Soh, Kien & Tay-Yap, 2000). The systemic character, the procedural logic and the overall outlook of ERP packages as described above cannot be undone through contextual adaptation. The technical terms of *reconfiguration* and *parameterization* commonly deployed in this context bespeak the limited adaptation of ERP packages to local contexts; as both operations are performed upon an anterior structure of data items and relations. Indeed, it may be conjectured that the rituals surrounding the implementation of an ERP package (see, e.g., Avital & Vandenbosch, 2000) are by and large oriented towards transcribing the reality of particular organizations into the language of the package rather than the other way around (Pollock, Williams & Procter, 2003). Complex as it may be, the implementation process whereby ERP packages are changed or adapted to local contexts is subject to polyvalent constraints.

Postscript

In this chapter I have sought to unpack organization-wide, off-the-shelf information packages usually known as ERP systems and to disclose some of the organizational and behavioural premises on which they are predicated. I have in particular claimed that packages of this sort conceive transactions (simple, routine and well defined tasks) as the elementary building blocks of organizations. Made in principle of such simple and well-defined tasks, organizational operations can be mapped onto software and conducted as large series of largely automated operations. The carrying out of these operations benefits from the links ERP packages encode across and within organizational functions and processes and the technological innovations (modular architecture and database management) they have relied upon to support such cross-functional processes.

I have furthermore claimed that the commercially available ERP packages are based on the standard functional structural template of organization whereby most tasks are grouped into functions and sub-functions. The limitations of the functional structure have been vividly debated in organization theory and management studies (e.g., Chandler, 1962, 1977; Mintzberg, 1979) but have not been given specific attention in the literature on ERP packages. Both the functional structure and the transactional logic on which ERP packages are based combine with the comprehensive character of these packages to impede the external orientation of operations conducted by means of the package. Contrary to the official rhetoric of market adaptation and business processes, the accommodation of the large number of internal operational links spins out a thick transactional texture that by implication perplexes the road to the market.

The conception of organizations in these terms is an example of the logic of functional simplification that I have described in Chapter 2, so essential to any attempt to entrust the carrying out of operations conducted by humans to machines. The functional simplification is produced by abstracting the logic and structure of the package from the complexity of the task environment within which these operations are normally conducted. It is easy to overlook in this regard that organizations are not merely transactional assemblies but complex social institutions in which the distribution and carry out of duties reflect a variety of experiences, skills and preoccupations (Kallinikos, 2006; March & Olsen, 1989).

It is this multidimensional character of social practice that becomes simplified and reduced to transactions that can be embedded into software. While these premises underlie any software, the distinguishing attribute of ERP packages consists of the fact that they target the entire gamut of operations of organizations. The far-reaching implications such packages have, often unacknowledged in the literature, relate to their inclusiveness and the fact that they are potent instruments for erasing or marginalizing other modes of engaging with the world that do not conform with the linear logic which such packages embody. This claim provides another set of reasons as to why empirical studies of ERP packages must extend beyond the time-limited horizons of most case studies and the localist bias they tend to exhibit. The long-lasting effects, which the diffusion of such packages brings about, demand a multi-sited ethnography with enduring involvement in the field, capable of disclosing different modes of engaging with the world and the conflicts thus engendered (Pollock & Williams, 2009; Zuboff, 1988).

I have mentioned several times the conception of human agency in transactional terms that ERP packages embody and the understanding of human agency as the enactment of pre-arranged sequences of steps, that is, a procedure. I turn in the next chapter to the exploration of some of the behavioural implications such an understanding and instrumentation of human agency are bound to bring about.

5
Addendum on the Behavioural Implications of Information Packages

Human agency as procedure enactment

In this chapter, I pursue in some detail the exploration of some of the behavioural implications of ERP packages. It would seem fairly reasonable to conjecture that the elaborate depiction of organizational relations that these packages mediate frames the perception of relevant events and the modes whereby duties are carried out. Broadly speaking, acting upon the world is closely associated with the context in which one's actions are placed and the demands or opportunities inferred from reading that context (Goffman, 1974; Weick, 1993). It also depends on the resources at one's own disposal, prescriptive orders and structural constraints as well as the models of acting that prevail in one's own environment. ERP packages have a part to play in all these situations.

The claims put forth in the preceding chapter suggest that the implications of ERP packages reach far beyond the officially acclaimed goal of rendering the organizational operations ordered, visible and integrated. By providing the infrastructural means for tracing cause–effect, means–ends relationships across the organization, ERP packages assist in constructing a manageable/predictable organizational reality. At the same time, ERP packages fashion trails of action, that is, elaborate procedural schemes whereby the execution and monitoring of a task or group of tasks are pursued. As claimed in Chapter 2, a distinctive characteristic of all technologies is precisely the reshaping of human contributions through functional simplification, closure and automation. In this respect, ERP technology resembles any other technology. It codifies routine or semi-routine operations and standardizes their execution by entrusting a considerable part of that execution to machines.

However, unlike other less encompassing software packages, the conception of organizational operations as an extended sequence of discrete steps establishes a long-driven 'behavioural mechanics' throughout the organization. In dissecting organizational operations in discrete items and providing the procedural sequences for the execution of particular tasks, encompassing computer-based applications such as ERP packages engrave the paths along which human contributions are expected to unfold. They therefore assist in setting up patterns of action and communication and in shaping human agency in organizations. It is important to understand the distinctive mode whereby packages of this nature shape human behaviour. By way of contrast to expert systems, ERP technology does not target knowledge and modes of inference, at least not predominantly, but rather *procedures of action and execution schemes.*[1] The introduction of this family of technologies to organizations has therefore less sophisticated goals than the computer-based codification of expert behaviour. ERP packages are simply concerned with the procedural standardization and computer-based instrumentation of an impressive array of organizational operations, a task that is rendered feasible through the expansion of these packages' application domain. In this manner, ERP systems become an important means for constructing governable and accountable patterns of behaviour in organizations along the lines suggested in Chapter 2 (see, also, Kallinikos, 1996; Miller & O'Leary, 1987, 1994).

Large-scale information packages cannot but construct modes of human involvement as they go about integrating organizational transactions. In other words, ERP packages carry performative implications, in the sense of defining items and discrete transactional acts and construing relations between them. In so doing, they combine them into extended sequences that are vested with a sort of purpose and direction. For instance, the buying of input materials through the system obeys a strict procedural order. This involves inspection of a number of relevant data items, the making of the final decision and the following up of the delivery, for example, checking available inventory, reviewing supplier catalogues, comparing prices and terms of delivery, ordering, following up delivery, etc. Most significantly, the procedural sequence now takes place with a clear awareness of the greater ecology of relations (e.g., accounting and finance, operations and warehouse management) upon which it tends to impinge, and which the

[1]The representation of knowledge (facts about the world) is key to expert systems. Inferences are simpler (logical modes) and their quality is crucially dependent on what is represented in the system (e.g., Dreyfus, 2001; Dreyfus & Dreyfus, 1986; Winograd, 1990). ERP packages are very different in this respect.

system renders visible and possible to inspect and trace at any moment. The influence of the system cannot therefore be gauged adequately in terms of support to the user. Rather, large-scale, proactively oriented systems, as those ERP packages exemplify, invite highly selective modes of participation (compliance to the procedural logic, the data items and transactions the system entails) that block and by implication eliminate (not many things can be accomplished without the system) alternative ways of doing things (Hasselbladh & Kallinikos, 2000). ERP packages in this manner regulate behaviour in the immediate way of preventing certain options (Grimmelmann, 2005) and though providing the infrastructural mechanics for pursuing organizational objectives.

ERP packages are therefore distinguished by the insertion of every transaction they help define or record into the wider ecology of organizational relations to which each transaction impinges or is linked to. By tying steps together and placing separate tasks and contributions within the wider context of other tasks or missions, ERP packages tend to markedly shape the building blocks of organizational action such as jobs, duties and roles. Rather than being simply descriptive, ERP packages are prescriptive or, as claimed above, performative in their orientation. That is, they do not simply automate and integrate transactions. In addition they frame the import such transactions may have by placing them in the wider organizational context to which the designers of the system construe they belong. The very meaning of 'best practices' on which ERP packages are claimed to be based indicates that the target of such packages are ways of doing rather than simply the codification, automation and integration of particular transactions.

The reconstruction and retracing of the interconnected nature of organizational tasks thus makes ERP technology capable of constructing extended action itineraries. Functional modules, sub-functional categories and cross-functional processes are not simply depictions of information flows but also and, perhaps predominantly, execution schemes. In this manner, ERP systems differ from traditional information systems but also the automated versions of human action we call 'expert' or 'decision-support' systems. They definitely entail the shaping of larger enclaves of tasks and provide the informational and transactional infrastructure upon which procedural modes of conduct are constituted.

Framing

The distinctive behavioural implications of ERP technology emerge against the background of the juxtaposition of human agency that takes the form of procedure with other modes of human involvement. A little while ago cognitive psychologist Anderson (1983) distinguished between *declarative knowledge* (knowledge about facts and relationships in a specific domain) and *procedural knowledge* (how-to-make-it knowledge), a distinction presumably akin to Ryle's (1949) widely acclaimed categories of *knowing what* and *knowing how*. Anderson claimed that the translation of declarative knowledge to procedural knowledge is a basic attribute of human behaviour. The transition to adulthood and the process of personal maturation involve not simply the acquisition of knowledge about the world but most decisively its transformation to procedural knowledge that provides the guidelines of how to handle particular situations. Professional training represents one of the clearest illustrations of this transformation (Dreyfus & Dreyfus, 1986). It shows how knowledge of facts and relationships in specific domains must be translated and ultimately evaluated on the efficacy of procedures for dealing with domain-specific problems.

The transformation of knowledge of facts and relationships into procedures is therefore a major accomplishment whereby humans become instrumental, test their knowledge of the world and understand the limits of that knowledge and its contextual embeddedness. In many respects this can be construed as fundamentally a pragmatist claim (James, 2000) in which embeddedness in a background of practice is juxtaposed with the detached perception and evaluation of courses of action.

However, the conversion of knowledge about the world to procedural knowledge takes many forms (Weick, 1979a, 1979b) and is just one of many paths that knowledge takes in its various transformations (Engestrom, 2001; Nonaka, 1994). The difference which ERP packages introduce relates not simply to the procedural translation of knowledge/ information but to the rigid separation of procedure from the decision of which procedure to enact. In resilient cognitive systems such as those humans represent, procedural knowledge is undergoing changes that may occasionally cause an understanding of the world in terms other than procedural. The confrontation with the world often involves procedure modification as response to changing facts, or as the outcome of a procedure's inadequacy to cope with the situation to which it has been regularly applied. Most significantly, the invocation of a procedure presupposes the tacit definition/reading of the situation (Goffman, 1974). Before humans enact a how-to-do-it knowledge, they have to frame the situation and decide what sort of behaviour it calls for, even though such framing may be provisional in unfamiliar situations or be made in conjunction to acting upon that situation (Weick, 1979b). In all these cases, backtracks and modifications and re-evaluation of committed courses of action remain possible alternatives.

Framing is a highly complex cognitive activity (Bateson, 1972; Goffman, 1974) that allows for the tuning or behaviour adaptation to the demands of particular situations. It cannot thus be separated, at least not without serious consequences, from the web of significations and the practices underlying a particular social context. Weick's (1993) analysis of the Mann Gulch disaster is instructive as to what may happen when framing or 'sense-making', as he calls it, collapses or becomes dissociated from action. Coping with urgent and ambiguous situations often presupposes the ability of responding innovatively to these situations. Such an ability, in turn, is inextricably bound up with the capacity of reading/framing such situations properly, testing the validity of that framing and taking corrective action if initial assumptions do not work well. Rigidly dissociated from framing, action loses its intentional component and tends to degenerate to mindless procedure of execution that may have devastating consequences, as the Mann Gulch disaster clearly demonstrates.

By inserting the enactment of a procedure within the ecology of organizational relations to which such a procedure is thought to belong, ERP systems basically dissolve the link between framing and action. In so doing, they force, wittingly or unwittingly, a 'behavioural mechanics' throughout the organization. Vendor evaluation, to refer to the same example again, is proceduralized by providing a number of steps that have to be followed and the criteria on the basis of which each step must be completed. The procedure obtains its meaning within the wider framework of materials management as codified by the system, the work performed by peers in adjacent or related positions (e.g., accounting, invoice verification), the values supplied by the very criteria of vendor evaluation the system provides, etc. There may be and usually is some leeway to manipulate these conditions, if experience shows the system to be inadequate, overconstraining or simply irrelevant.

However, significant lessons of experience can be fed back into the system only through periodic reconfigurations of the package. Of necessity this is done by actors other than those experiencing the limitations of the package. The procedure cannot be instantly modified, despite evidence suggesting particular situations to require a more or less different procedural treatment and other evaluation criteria. The demands of comprehensive automation/integration have drastically separated the activities of framing and procedure enactment. This contrasts with the aforementioned claims suggesting that the ability to evaluate procedural modes of acting cannot be accounted for by procedural knowledge itself. The very judgement of how well a procedure performs cannot be based on the procedure itself. It requires access to skills, significations, values (i.e., goals) and beliefs about the state of the world. In one way or another, knowledge about the world forms always the background against which procedural knowledge gains its meaning and usefulness (Bateson, 1972; Goffman, 1974; Lackoff, 1995).

There are other concerns about the rigid separation of framing from action that may inhibit learning and adaptive behaviour (Engestrom, 2001; Engestrom and Middleton, 1996). Habituation and the insights stemming from human embeddedness in the practical world (Dreyfus & Dreyfus, 1986; Introna & Whitley, 2000) contribute to the withdrawal of procedural skills from immediate inspection and deliberate manipulation. In this manner procedural knowledge melts into imagination and to the reservoir of knowledge about the world. Socialization and apprenticeship are further examples that Nonaka (1994) suggests exemplify the opposite journey, that is, the transformation of procedural knowledge into knowledge about the world. Both involve learning through demonstration, exemplification and rule or procedure-following. Overall, the complex ties between framing, acting and learning are considerably simplified by the very organizational/behavioural premises on which ERP packages are predicated. It is therefore crucial to uphold that the distinction between various forms of knowledge and the involvement they imply makes sense only in a cognitive system capable of sustaining the essential bonds between these two types of knowledge (Lackoff, 1995). Rigidly separated from one another, these basic human capabilities tend to degenerate to non-imaginative, mechanical ways of thinking and acting. The understanding of human agency as procedure enactment that ERP packages embody have thus profound implications for humans and organizations that go far beyond the official rhetoric of efficiency-seeking.

Modes of involvement

Let me not be misunderstood as trying to defend a vision of humanity which technology threatens. Benign as it may be, this is not my purpose in this volume. Obviously, the diffusion of machines and the procedures they help install at the heart of work, public and private life carry important implications that have to be scrutinized and possibly resisted or renegotiated. My purpose in this chapter is, however, narrower and aims at depicting some of the far-reaching behavioural consequences of the diffusion of large-scale information packages that have largely escaped the limelight. In so doing, I wish, of course, to amass evidence of the key claims made throughout this volume concerning the understanding of technology as regulative regime rather than simply a productive force and efficiency medium.

Sometime ago the renowned semiotician, Yuri Lotman, made a distinction between *grammar-oriented* and *text-oriented* cultures (see Eco, 1976). Broadly speaking, grammar-oriented cultures are characterized by the elaborate specification of rules on the basis of which appropriate modes of conduct are enacted as a means of coping with particular situations. Under such a cultural regime, human behaviour becomes relatively predictable. That is, people draw on this legible, as it were, normative stock of knowledge to invoke those rules that respond to the situations faced. By way of contrast, text-oriented cultures rely on socially diffused yet vaguely formulated ways of dealing with various situations. Rather than being codified in terms of rules, appropriate modes of conduct must be inferred/constructed each time out of the variety of cues and materials that assist in making sense of particular situations.

Though considerably broader in its reach, Lotman's distinction is akin to procedural versus less-structured forms of involvement with the world that I endeavoured to develop in this and the preceding chapter. The diffusion of ERP systems and their expanding organizational involvement participate in the making of formal organizations and social practice to grammar-oriented cultures, at the expense of other, less-structured modes of human behaviour at work. As noted above, ERP systems are prescriptive, setting up elaborate procedures by means of which an impressive variety of tasks are to be accomplished. Inscribed to such an elaborate regime of rules and procedures, human behaviour becomes less unpredictable while organizational reality emerges as transparent (i.e., adequately described in terms of information) and accountable (i.e., traceable in terms of who made what under which conditions). In this process, organizations might come to control their everyday operations better but they may as well end up loosing other important sources of innovation, learning and development (March, 1991).

The transactional mechanics, which ERP packages bring about, may thus block exploration of alternative ways of perceiving and acting upon reality and by extension organizational development and innovation (March, 1991). The opportunity to experiment, improvise and rehearse with alternative ways of perceiving and acting upon the world thus presupposes forms of human involvement that are sharply distinguished from human behaviour as rule-following. Such forms of human involvement, often revealed in improvisation (Ciborra, 1999; Weick, 1979a, 1993) and play (Bateson, 1972; Kallinikos, 1996), collapse the distinction between general and procedural knowledge, knowing *what* and knowing *how*. They ceaselessly trade off one for another as a way of dealing with shifting states of the world and learning about it. Most significantly, they break with the sequential pattern of procedural action and its linear imposition of a temporal order. In improvisation and play, the world is revealed in its holistic and synthetic particularity, entailing flashes of insight into how things are tied together (Bateson, 1972; Erikson, 1977). Procedural knowledge is of course implicated in these basic forms of involvement, yet never as a separate realm of human agency.

Some of the claims I make in this chapter could presumably be associated with those concerns Lamb and Kling (2003) have raised around the notion of the user, underlying much of the information systems research and practice. Lamb and Kling question the rationalistic underpinnings and the cognitive individualism implicit in the notion of the user. They argue instead that social actors, using information and communication technologies, find often themselves embedded in complex networks of considerable social and technical complexity. They draw accordingly on several resources and enact multiple and shifting roles and competencies to cope with the complex situations facing them. The dominant notion of the user involves an utter simplification of this complex reality and requires drastic reconceptualization. In an analogous fashion, the behavioural presuppositions onto which ERP systems are predicated recount a rather simplistic conception of human behaviour that certainly reflects the inheritance of cognitive rationalism and the dominant position it has assumed in software engineering and information systems research and practice.

Postscript

The deconstruction of the ERP packages I have pursued in this and the preceding chapter may not deny any positive effects they may have on work and organizational life. Technologically supported procedure development and standardization that are based on best practices can break with the languid forms of contextual learning, introduce and condense lessons of experience to particular organizations and contribute to the efficient management of their operations. Also, the comprehensive, organization-wide character of ERP packages represents an essential means to the better coordination of organizational operations across functions and production sites. But there are significant behavioural and organizational side affects too that have by and large been overlooked. The procedural standardization brought about by ERP packages delineates a distinctive form of human involvement as procedure enactment. By the same token, procedural standardization contributes to the transformation of organizational practices to procedures. Standard operating procedures are ubiquitous in organizations and procedural skills and knowledge essential to human agents. However, their usefulness derives from the multiple connections they entertain with other forms of knowledge and modes of involvement (Pentland & Feldman, 2005). Technological embodiment of procedures by necessity loosens these connections. It cuts off procedure development from vital sources of knowledge and practice (e.g., tacit forms of knowledge, intuition, playful exploration and improvisation) that support and give meaning to procedures and makes it increasingly difficult to accommodate other forms of organizing experience.

Placed in this context, ERP systems strike a new balance in the delicate equilibrium of modes of human involvement and forms of knowledge that have been accommodating organizations in modern times. They privilege procedural knowledge and skills (an instance of general and codified knowledge) over other, mostly local, forms of knowledge and modes of involvement. They put a premium on control, efficiency and standardization and inevitably subordinate issues of exploration and innovation in organizations (March, 1991). ERP technology is a technology of regulation not of innovation and must ultimately be evaluated against the background of the variety of organizational and human trade-offs it cannot help but bring into being. Now, the growing significance of the Internet, and novel developments both in the designing methodologies of ERP packages (e.g., component based methodologies) and in the forms of data/communication (multimedia and media convergence) that they can accommodate may change ERP packages from transactional/procedural machines into information infrastructures supporting a variety of modes of human involvement. I have deliberately left these issues outside of consideration, focusing instead on depicting the distinctive forms whereby ERP systems restructure work and organizational processes. It remains to be seen what sort of effects these new developments may have but I predict that the transactional/procedural legacy of ERP packages will persist in one form or another and be further diffused by the ubiquitous presence of information artefacts and the Internet in nearly all walks of life.

6
Control and Complexity in a Connected World

The mixed blessings of connectedness

Information is the cognitive currency of the age. Diffused across the social fabric by a wide and growing range of information systems and artefacts, information is variously involved in the making and monitoring of such diverse institutions such as formal organizations, professions, markets, mass media or politics. Such a state of affairs bespeaks not simply the greater leeway information continues to command in the making of human affairs. It also suggests that technological information is not just a means, no matter how ubiquitous, in the service of pre-established ends but a major force of organizational and institutional change. Strong or trivial as it may seem, such a claim must though be restated clearly, in view of a wide-spread distrust against categorical statements that attribute a causal status to technology.[1]

The momentum information and information technologies continue to acquire in the contemporary world is manifested, among other things, in the growing interlocking and standardization (a prerequisite for interlocking) of the rapidly expanding population of information-based systems and artefacts. The construction of a relatively standardized and navigable infospace within and across organizations and regions would appear to inaugurate a distinct stage in the contemporary technology's involvement in socio-economic life. For all its significance, information that remains locally confined cannot respond to the challenge of a market-oriented, global world. Locally produced information requires to be communicated, transferred and processed, rapidly and effectively, within and across organizations, contexts of practice

[1]See, for example, Arnold (2003), Cutcliffe and Mitcham (2001), Orlikowski (2000), Woolgar (2002).

and regions, and over time. The diffusion of information standards across industries and regions can be seen as a response to the challenge which the traffic of information across the limited horizons of local contexts posits. As standards are negotiated and diffuse, they tend to establish the technical requirements for global systems of information-handling, exchange and communication (Bowker & Star, 1999; Zittrain, 2008). The Internet is the most conspicuous and global manifestation of these developments but many other less encompassing local or function-based networks also exist. At the same time, the organizational deployment of large-scale information packages such as Enterprise Resource Planning Systems (ERP) or Customer Relationship Management Systems (CRM) make their own contribution to the unification of the information habitat of organizations. As shown in the preceding two chapters, commercial, off-the-shelf packages of this sort assist in disseminating similar information structures and processes across organizations, functions and regions (Kallinikos, 2004b).

These developments suggest that information technologies bring together aspects of the world that had previously remained unrelated in terms of function or locality. The positive outcomes of an interconnected world, manifested in the rapid and effective processing and transfer of information across organizational, institutional and geographical boundaries are rather conspicuous to require lengthy treatment in this context (see, e.g., Benkler, 2006; Castells, 1996, 2001). But encompassing processes of this type hardly remain univocal in their consequences. There is the widely acknowledged theme of unintended consequences of intentional action, so well epitomized by the food and pharmaceutical industries or the wider environmental effects of industrial technologies (Beck, 1992). That theme resonates with the putative involvement of information technologies in the recurring financial turmoil of the past decade. There is by now significant evidence that shows the widespread diffusion of side effects in the connected world of the information age. Electronic 'identity' theft and fraud, the diffusion of malicious software, Internet-mediated pornography and electronic crime in general are some conspicuous unintended consequences brought about by the global interlocking of information-based systems and artefacts (Johnson & Nissenbaum, 1995; Zittrain, 2008). However, there may also be others that live a more surreptitious life and can be identified by the lens of critical analytic deconstruction.

The interconnectedness which contemporary technologies of information and communication help to bring to being challenges a longstanding tradition, and perhaps wisdom, of control (Foucault, 1977). Keeping things separate avoids messing them up and provides some inspection and control over people and things, and the interactive processes taking place between them. The interactions, in particular, between previously unrelated processes or functionalities may set out a dynamics with unforeseen results. In some cases, integration may unwittingly undo defence mechanisms that secure the smooth function of the processes or systems involved or simply provide new opportunities that can be used in adverse ways, as most electronic crime exemplifies (Hanseth & Ciborra, 2007). In other cases, integration may export or recreate risk at a more inclusive level trading off high frequency with high-impact risks, a condition of which current financial crises are perhaps a poignant reminiscence.

Given the standardized and navigable nature of the information environment, negative effects following one or another incidence that were before locally contained may rapidly propagate across the now interconnected networked space. 'Ill will has become more potent and destructive' in a connected world, Borgmann (1999, p. 196) claims. In such a context, the old but reliable strategy of coping with threats or dangers by isolating them may not be easily applicable. Control is, after all, an exercise in boundary-drawing and boundary management. In his acclaimed study of 'normal accidents' Perrow (1986) demonstrates that interconnectedness brings mixed blessings. While often enabling, interconnectedness may too raise the complexity of the interacting components and cause unintended and, occasionally, deeply regretful consequences. Indeed, Perrow suggests that accidents of this nature are unavoidable (hence the term 'normal accidents') in tightly interconnected or dense/concentrated systems, whose components may involve non-linear, and, for this reason, hardly predictable forms of causality.

In other words, the pervasive character of the emerging interconnected information environment reframes some of the dominant strategies of technological control that have been manifested in the construction of largely self-contained or, at least, largely independent technological systems. An appreciation of what such a reframing may entail, necessitates the analytical treatment of the distinct forms whereby technology has traditionally been involved in the construction of predictable worlds. Such an analysis therefore helps disclose the ways whereby current technological developments challenge traditional strategies of technological control (e.g., interconnectedness versus loose coupling) and the organizational practices commonly associated with them.

Attributing such significance to the reframing of the traditional strategies of technological control, which current developments signify, may need motivation. A widespread assumption is evident in the literature that information-based systems and artefacts change the transactional architecture of social interaction and, in so doing, alter some of the premises on which traditional organizational forms have been predicated (e.g., Castells, 1996; Knorr-Cetina & Brugger, 2002). Besides being rather vague, such an assumption has often assumed the status of an unquestioned axiom. With perhaps few exceptions (e.g., Arthur, 2009; Beniger, 1986; Luhmann, 1993), theories of how information and the technologies whereby it is supported are involved in the remaking of the traditional premises of technological control have been rare.

In what follows, I seek to develop the theoretical claims that depict the distinct forms whereby technology has traditionally been involved in the making and regulation of human affairs. In so doing, I draw heavily on Luhmann (1993) and I reframe his conception of technology as *functional simplification and closure* presented in Chapter 2. Whereas in Chapter 2 I sought to discover the potency of technology as key governance regime of social practice, here I place greater emphasis on the structural or organizational implications of technology and how dominant forms of organizing social practice (e.g., formal organizations) can be traced back to, or in any case be strongly related to, bounded technological systems and the concentrated nature of organizational arrangements associated with such systems. In this regard, Luhmann's account of technology is particularly germane for assessing some of the implications that are associated with the growing interlocking of information systems and artefacts. Such an account helps provide the conceptual background against which contemporary technological developments contrast with the traditional strategies of technological control.

The system of technology

A widespread intellectual habit conceives technology in instrumental terms as just a means deployed to increase the effectiveness of human operations. Hardly contestable as it may be, the understanding of technology in terms of means–ends recounts one aspect of a much more multifaceted phenomenon. It tends to put the emphasis on the very ends technology is called upon to serve and thus overlooks the distinctive forms and patterns whereby technology is involved in the accomplishment of these ends. There is 'how' in addition to 'what', and the making and regulation of those practices, goals or operations that technology is supposed to serve is crucial for assessing its social and material implications.

Any system of considerable complexity never addresses the world (the domain it bears upon) in a straightforward fashion. This is not possible as the system has to accommodate its internal organization of elements, components or processes that constitute it as a particular system. Even simple devices (rather than technological systems) such as a mobile telephone or an iPod mediate the world through the tasks and operations that are intrinsic to them. There is therefore no system (technological or otherwise) without some form of self-reference that derives from the need of reproducing its internal operations. An artefact that does not do so is simply broken or dysfunctional. Even language/speech, as is seen in more detail in the next two chapters, is required to arrange its terms (articles, nouns, verbs, adjectives) in forms that obey the rules of grammar and syntax, which ultimately boils down to the internal accommodation of each of the terms by the others (Barthes, 1967; Eco, 1976).

Drawing on Luhmann (1993), I portray technology as a *structural form* deployed to manage an unpredictable world. The key problem technology resolves is the control of contingencies that beset all human action in modern world. Viewed in this manner, technology emerges as a standardized and closed arrangement of artefacts/processes designed and deployed to produce a minimum platform of predictable relations, in an otherwise shifting and contingent world (Bloomfield & Vurdubakis, 2001). As I claimed in the previous chapters, the *geist* of technology is revealed in its reifying strategies. Or, in Latour's much-quoted phrase, 'technology is society made durable'. Any reliable technological system is expected to function in a largely recurrent fashion over time and across contexts and in this manner contingencies are managed or avoided. The standardized and recurrent status of technological operations does not deny the variety of purposes to which any particular technology can be called upon to serve. Indeed, and, contrary to a widespread misconception, standardization (a successful reification) is essential to contextual adaptation. The frustration caused by technological devices that fail to deliver on their promise is a poignant reminder of the complex relationship standardization entertains with human purpose and contextual adaptation. Reflection on language and other resilient and highly flexible systems of human-making suggests that a certain degree of standardization is essential for sustaining purposeful activity (Bolter, 1991; Ong, 1982; Mumford, 1952).

The instrumentation of standardized, quasi-predictable relations is accomplished by the twin strategy of *functional closure* and *simplification* (Luhmann, 1993). Functional simplification or *funktionierende simpifizierung*[2]

---

[2]The German term alludes to the dynamic character of this process. To translate literally, however, to the English correspondence 'functioning simplification' would have been awkward and perhaps slightly misleading.

involves the demarcation of an operational domain, within which the complexity of the world is reconstructed as a simplified set of causal or instrumental relations. These last can be quite complex in themselves and their causal force significantly magnified, for example, nuclear power, process technologies, freeway traffic systems. However, due to the initial reduction of the factors involved, the relative processes remain potentially inspectable and controllable, whereas the knowledge on which they are made possible allows for the accomplishment of these goals. Functional closure, on the other hand, implies the construction of a protective cocoon that is placed around the selected causal sequences or processes to safeguard undesired interference and ensure their recurrent unfolding. Functional simplification and closure implicate one another and straightforwardly express, as Luhmann claims, the *geist* of technology in modern times The predictable forms whereby technology often (but not always) operates are precisely due to the construction of simplified or planned causalities, whose recurrent unfolding is ensured through the exclusion (or the attempt to such an exclusion) of any possible factor that could impinge on and disturb such a functionally simplified order.

Abstract as it may be, such an account of technology is well captured in the widely used engineering term 'blackboxing'. It is also re-encountered across a number of authoritative texts on organizations (e.g., Mintzberg, 1979; Thompson, 1967). Whereas the pattern of causal sequences may vary (e.g., pooled, serial and reciprocal patterns of interdependencies), organizations construct the protective cocoon of technology by the closed loops of technological sequences. They further re-enhance technological closure through extensive reliance on such methods as forecasting, stockpiling, procedural control of inputs and other kinds of buffer (Thompson, 1967). All these methods and techniques aim to ensure the undisturbed unfolding of technological sequences. Closure or blackboxing by definition implies the very decoupling of the operations of the technical system from the wider organizational and social relations within which such a system is embedded. Social contact with technological process is highly regulated through prescriptions, the specification of skill profiles and requirements and role formation. Technological and organizational designs thus make abundant use of local containment, separation and loose coupling as basic strategies of control (Perrow, 1984; Weick, 1976).

The understanding of technology as a system that is predicated on the principles of functional simplification and closure could be said to derive predominantly from the industrial experience. Cognitive systems such as those constructed or enabled by computer-based technology are premised upon differences (binary alterations) rather than material causes (Bateson, 1972).

The conception of technology as a system premised on functional simplification and closure has therefore to be modified to account for the cognitive, sign-based constitution of information technology. In this last case, causal simplification and closure take the form of *procedural standardization* and *cognitive closure*. The software of hardware entails elaborate systems of rules and procedures on the basis of which symbol or information tokens and the cognitive relations they mediate are established and manipulated. The functionality of particular programs is accomplished through the painstaking elaboration of the steps involved, and the closed loops by which such steps are combined to fixed sequences.

Procedural standardization is essential to software technology. As shown in the previous two chapters, large-scale information systems exemplify well the logic of procedural standardization at several levels. Monitoring of customers through CRM always entails a number of steps whereby the customer's profile is constructed. Such steps may ramify to various aspects of organizational life but they are always tied to procedural sequences and combinations whereby profiling techniques are constructed. For instance, customer's buying and paying behaviour is decomposed into various steps, assigned to predefined categories and regrouped by recourse to combinatorial rules to construct the relevant profile. In a similar fashion, logistic operations mediated by ERP packages are organized as a large series of steps that ramify into cross-functional operations, for example, materials management, finance and accounting, warehouse management. Such steps are tied to procedural sequences that define a greater task, for example, the task of buying is sequenced as following: reviewing materials, checking price, quality and delivery conditions, making a choice, placing the order, receiving invoice, making the payment, follow-up the product delivery, etc. (Kallinikos, 2004b). Automated rules and procedures extend, of course, far beyond the human interface which these examples concern. Operating at that interface is made possible by means of a deeper and more comprehensive automation through which information items either as symbol tokens (software) or electronic signals (hardware) are manipulated (Kallinikos, 2009a; Manovich, 2001). Elaborate, automated rules for processing data are, for instance, necessary to retrieve data from the repositories in which they are stored as means of accomplishing tasks at the interface.

A case could accordingly be made for the fact that the functional simplification in the case of software technology entails the careful demarcation of an operational domain (i.e., the functionality of the program), the definition of the tasks that embody the functionality of the program and the lay out of the steps that have to be followed in order to accomplish a task or series of tasks. The program itself may be quite complex but the tasks it performs have been substantially cleared up from ambiguities, and their execution standardized in an elaborate system of procedures.

The brilliant analysis of the limitations of the Von Neumannian games once performed by Bateson (1972) is instructive for understanding the nature of the functional simplification/closure underlying particular programs. The problem with the Von Neumann's 'player', Bateson (1972, pp. 285–7) noted, is that it cannot learn from experience. Negative outcomes that are due to the 'player's' misperception of the confronted relationships cannot be fed back into the cognitive reorganization of the 'player'. The mathematical fiction the 'player' is will perform exactly the same way (dictated by the abstract and general character of mathematical relations the model of the 'player' epitomizes) in the next encounter. Unforeseen relations cannot be handled *in situ*. They could possibly be incorporated into the model by the programmer, in a future periodic revision of the model, but the 'player' itself cannot respond contingently. Functional simplification is precisely manifested in the closed loops the program performs, the implicit conduit metaphor upon which software engineering is predicated (Lackoff, 1995). The learning algorithms currently constructed by the technology of neural networks do not radically alter this situation, even though they claim to do so. They just push it one step back on the procedural standardization of the learning mechanism which is but an algorithm (Ekbia, 2008; Hayles, 2005; Kallinikos, 1998).[3]

The algorithmic constitution of programs thus suggests that the technological goals of recurrence and predictability of information-based artefacts are accomplished through the selection and standardization of the cognitive operations the program entails, and their procedural execution. Automation of procedures and rules ensure the procedural standardization and cognitive closure of the program and correspond, by and large, to the Luhmannian concepts of functional simplification and closure. Functional closure is furthermore accomplished through the specification of the information requirements (the program admits only certain inputs), various forms that regulate access to the program, cryptography, protocols and other security mechanisms that function as a kind of protective cocoon.

---

[3] This claim raises some intricate and central questions in Artificial Intelligence that in the end call for the explication of what we mean by humans and human learning. For obvious reasons I cannot discuss these questions here.

Such an account of technology may strike latecomers in constructivism/ interpretivism as utterly devoid of humans and marked by a strong flavour of determinism. Whatever 'determinism' means, it has been a negative word for at least the past two decades. While I raised serious concerns in previous chapters as to the rhetorical use of the term 'determinism' and the alternatives that the debunking of the term is supposed to enable, a few clarifying comments may be suitable here. The understanding of the forms whereby technology influences human choice can never be exhausted at the human-technology interface, no matter how compelling this may be felt to be (Borgmann, 1984). Not only is technology structurally complex, as I have claimed above, technologies are in addition embedded in complex social and historical patterns that reach far beyond their situated use (Misa, Brey & Feenberg, 2003; Pinch, 2008). Most significantly, technologies participate in constituting aspects of human agency through extensive training, education and practice formation (Kallinikos, 2002, 2004c; Pinch, 2008). To treat functional closure and simplification (i.e., blackboxing) as determinist is to miss completely the point concerning the *distinctive forms* whereby technology is involved in human affairs. Distinctiveness, it should be noted, does not imply an appeal to a 'technical bottom line' kind of argument (Knights et al., 2002). Functional closure and simplification are not causes but formative contexts (Ciborra & Lanzara, 1994), socially constructed, under particular regimes of knowledge, and with the view to serving specific goals, interests, values or preoccupations. Their operations are similarly supported through routines, standard operating procedures and organizational models or practices that reflect wider forms of social learning but also the experience of the very contexts in which technologies find themselves embedded.

Functional closure and simplification vary significantly from technology to technology and so do the forms whereby various technologies admit or invite human participation/intervention. Mobile devices, for instance, may differ from ERP systems in the manner in which they embody the strategies of functional simplification and closure. It is a crucial task of the social study of technology to disclose and reconstruct the ensemble of both wider societal and context-embedded factors that account for these differences and the role technology plays in that game. This is the point made by authors with different ontological preferences and paradigmatic attachments.[4] Unless placed, in its proper context, the concept and antidote to

---

[4] See, for example, Borgmann (1984, 1992), Hughes (1987), Kling (1992), Luhmann (1993, 1995), Mumford (1934, 1952), Winner (1977, 1993), Perrow (1967, 1986) to name but a few.

determinism known as *interpretive flexibility* (Bijker, Hughes & Pinch, 1987; Bijker, 2001) may well lead to a sort of contextual relativism, that in the end undoes and renders superfluous the very concept of technology (Strathern, 2002). If technology is infinitely malleable and contextually configurable then why bother analysing its implications? All we are required to study is the context of social relations in which it is embedded. If, on the other hand, the contextual assimilation of technology is partly controlled by the complex and time-evolving strategies of objectification that artefacts embody, then these strategies need to be exposed to critical interrogation that helps disclose the distinctive forms whereby technology may participate in the making of human affairs.

Limits to control: Self-reinforcing complexity

For all its difference to industrial technology, the principles of cognitive/ semantic closure and procedural standardization underlying computer programs/software packages recount the basic strategy whereby technology in general attempts to deal with the contingent character of the world (Bloomfield & Vurdubakis, 2001). Computer programs embody clear rules of reality representation and automated procedures of information-processing and inference-making (Zuboff, 1988). In so doing, they participate in the reproduction of an order in roughly similar ways to those Luhmann (1993) subsumes under the labels of 'functional simplification' and 'closure'. That is, they guarantee the recurrence of the operations internal to the system, while their interface with the reality external to the program takes place along highly selective paths (i.e., strict input requirements, formation of skill and role profiles, security arrangements) that ensure the reproduction of the program's operations through the exclusion of unwanted interference.

Frequent technological failures and malfunctioning (Perrow, 1984) suggest, however, that the project of functional simplification and closure is but partly achieved. The control of the internal loops that make up the system is never complete while the risk of external interference can be reduced but never eliminated. Contingent events that manage to intrude the closed circuits of technological interactions may cause significant problems and, at times, wreak havoc as they may ride on the intensified/magnified nature of these interactions. Technologically induced accidents give an indication of the magnified forces that under adverse conditions manage to escape technological control. The pattern is well known: functional simplification and closure enable the magnification of the causal or instrumental processes involved. But once the closed circuit of technological processes is broken, the forces that are set free often have grave or even devastating effects. Nuclear accidents stand as the epitome here. A less dramatic and instructive example is provided by freeway traffic systems. The functional simplification of driving conditions and the closure from other external interference enable the high-speed traffic of huge number of cars. Owing to traffic magnification, however, malfunctioning or disturbances in freeway traffic usually produce grave consequences in the form of long traffic delays (i.e., huge car queues) caused by the time-consuming effort to bring the system back to its normal functioning.

These observations suggest that the unexpected events that manage to intrude the closed circuits of technological systems cannot be coped with by the intrinsically blind character of technological sequences, at the very level which these sequences operate. Additional, ancillary mechanisms, ranging from routine safety tests to contingency plans, must be added to the system, initiating a vicious circle of increasing complexity, which the system initially set out to combat (Luhmann, 1993). The forces or processes that, through the strategies of functional simplification and closure, have been placed outside the technological system threaten to return and unsettle its operations. They stand as an imminent danger which must be coped with, through the careful reintroduction of complexity, annexed onto the core processes of the system in the form of safety or security mechanisms. The flipside of technological simplification is *loss of flexibility and contingent response* that have to be re-instituted through artificial mechanisms. Technological sequences cannot handle (i.e., absorb, ignore, forget or dissimulate) unforeseen incidents at the level on which they operate, even though technologists currently attempt to construct systems that respond to emergent events on the basis of learning from experience (i.e., neural networks). Such simple behavioural characteristics as forgetfulness, dissimulation and indifference that we often assume to be part and parcel of the limitations of humans, play an extremely important and adaptive role under conditions of emergence, complexity and unpredictability (Bateson, 1972; Luhmann, 1993; March, 1988).

While representing a major means for managing complexity, the technological strategies of functional simplification and closure are therefore subject to severe limits. Most crucial among them are the incapacity of a technological system thus constructed to deal with intruding and unexpected contingencies, and the consequent need to pre-program how such an intrusion, if and when it takes place, should be dealt with. But it belongs to the nature, as it were, of contingency (as disasters and accidents so well demonstrate) to be only modestly managed through antecedent preparation. Further, there are limits, as we endeavour to show in the next section, to how much complexity can be reintroduced into the system in the form of ancillary security mechanisms. It is therefore no surprise that failing functional simplification and closure may bring consequences of one or another kind, some of which may indeed be grave. Luhmann (1993) sorts these effects into three groups:

- *Chaos effects*, i.e., locally produced incidences of often minor character may disseminate rapidly across the entire system and trigger unpredictable chain effects wrecking havoc. Catastrophes such as those exemplified by aeroplane crashes, nuclear power or chemical industry accidents may well conform to the pattern of chaos effects. Similar effects may be less dramatic in tightly connected information systems but they can still bring serious economic consequences as they may seriously inhibit intra- and inter-organizational transactions. In cases in which information-based systems are deployed to monitor complex physical processes, as it now happens in aircraft or submarine navigation, nuclear power installations, etc., the effects may though be far-reaching and devastating.
- *Interference effects*, i.e., hardly predictable effects created by human intervention. Once manifested, effects of this nature are subject to learning (e.g., industrial pollution, negative effects of X-rays or antibiotics) and the operations of technology could eventually be readjusted to accommodate at least some of these effects. Issues relating to information overload, the management of junk email or software virus spreading, or the lessons taught by the dotcom fever could perhaps be thought as analogous phenomena in the age of information.
- *One-off incidences* of unique and haphazard nature not straightforwardly subject to learning.

Beyond functional simplification and closure

To recapitulate and extend: contemporary technologies of information and communication are deployed to render the operations that are brought to bear upon more predictable and manageable. They do so along lines that by and large recount the project of functional simplification and closure. However, in doing so, they too increase complexity in the form of an increasing interconnectedness between systems and applications but also through a recursive process whereby technologies of higher order (meta-technologies) are gradually added to take care of unforeseen incidents or forces that manage to pierce through the closed circuit of technological sequences. These developments accentuate the limitations to control accomplished through functional simplification and closure. Let me elaborate.

The reduction of complexity through the deployment of information-based systems often drives or 'exports' the handling of contingencies at a more inclusive level, in a roughly similar fashion to that presented above in connection with ancillary security arrangements. Owing to their communicative nature, information-based systems and artefacts often assume the role of a *meta-technology* controlling other technologies. They do so either in the form of providing straightforwardly security arrangements controlling the traffic of people and resources or through the planning and monitoring of technological operations (e.g., process industries, aircraft navigation, nuclear power generation). In other instances, information technology emerges as a primary technology, restructuring, regulating and monitoring processes that were previously performed in various, loosely coupled settings, in which a variety of technologies, practices and often organizations have been involved (e.g., bank and insurance offices, tax authorities, public e-procurement systems, etc.). In all or, at least, most of these circumstances, information and the technologies whereby it is supported become central media for compressing risks and transporting them to a more comprehensive level. The common, and from a point of view reasonable, assumption is that the superior information-processing and controlling capacity of information technology furnishes the means for spotting and adequately handling local failures, deviations or intruding contingencies. But there are side effects and unintended consequences and is important to understand how these may arise.

The rule so far has been that second-order (often security arrangements) mechanisms must be added to any technological system, to take care of unforeseen incidents. But these second-order technologies cannot but be themselves based on the principles of functional simplification and closure (Luhmann, 1993). For, second-order, safety technologies cannot but be constructed on the basic of conjectures about possible incidents and dysfunctions and this also applies to information technologies. By definition, they entail a fixed set of responses that could be invoked to cope with disruptive effects, as these last have been envisaged at the moment safety technology was designed. But if second-order technologies cannot control themselves, their possible failing must be controlled either by third-order technologies or other means that may involve direct human involvement. The growth of information-based security devices over the past decade suggests the control of technology through technology to be a tempting and perhaps unavoidable way forward.[5]

A complex technical scaffold is often the outcome of these processes, where second-order technologies control primary processes, tertiary technologies control security mechanisms of the second order and so forth. But, as indicated above, this technological scaffold must be constructed in advance and 'spot' responses specified and pre-programmed. The handling of contingencies and the risks such handling implicates are compressed into a complex net or hierarchy of technologies with the consequence of possible, large-scale disruptive effects (Borgmann, 1999). It may seem as a paradox yet control is a double-edged process that both increases (in some respects) and decreases (in some other respects) safety. Luhmann (1993, pp. 92–3) refers to the German romantic poet, Holderlin, to make the point that the quest of control may end up increasing rather than reducing risks.[6] I myself would like to recall the old maxim of Heraclitus that 'the same road that goes up goes also down'.

The disruptive effects of what is here construed as 'scaffold' collapse are often modest and represent perhaps a hybrid of the first two types of effect described by Luhmann (i.e., chaos and interference effects). Examples represent servers that break down (and this happens not infrequently), leaving considerable number of people idle for hours or days, or forcing them to revert to old ways of doing things, which may not be entirely possible either. The year-2000 (or millennium) problem may be a distant memory. Yet this problem is reminiscent of the risk and huge impact that the technological cascade I describe here may have, because intrinsic to such a strategy are the compression and transference of risks to a more inclusive level at which low-impact/high-frequency risk is traded off with high-impact/low-frequency risks.

A different technological landscape with a different kind of problem is gradually been formed by the very *connectivity* or *interoperability* contemporary technologies of information and communication are currently able to construct. Perhaps more than complexity, associated with the cascade of technologies into an encompassing order (first, second and third order technologies), connectivity and interoperability more straightforwardly challenge technological control accomplished through functional simplification and closure. For a variety of reasons, traditional technologies have, as a rule,

---

[5] In many cases security arrangements are as elaborate as the core functionality of the system or application which they bear upon.

[6] Wo aber Kontrolle ist/Wachst das Risiko auch (But where there is control/Risk grows as well).

remained functionally incompatible, for example, rail, air or road-traffic systems. Each one of them usually represents a cumulative strategy of problem-solving applied to a particular set of problems. TV sets, for instance, do not interact with other domestic electric appliances, freeway or railway systems embody different techniques and principles of transportation. Under these conditions functional complementarity (rather than interoperability) is accomplished by allowing one system to take over at the operational boundaries of the other (e.g., rail and air traffic). Traditional technologies seldom intersect or merge functionally, as they have been constructed by recourse to different principles and goals. In some cases, that is, subway and rail traffic, such functional merging may be an issue of appropriate standards. However, the self-contained nature of different technological systems often reflects widely different social and techno-scientific projects (e.g., air and rail traffic).

Information-based systems and technologies may also remain uncoupled or brought to bear upon one another through gateways and other similar techniques that translate data inputs back and forth from the one system to the other but leave the systems intact. Furthermore, technological path dependencies and lock-ins accentuate the need for backward and sideward compatible innovations, a process that is prone to create independent, self-reinforcing technological trajectories and fragmentation of information-based systems (Hanseth, 2000, 2004; Hanseth & Ciborra, 2007). In addition, a variety of social (e.g., exclusion) and institutional (e.g., firewalls) segmentations are imposed upon the Internet, making it a highly fragmented terrain (Sassen, 2004; Woolgar, 2002). The incompatibilities, divisions and segmentations that underlie both the Internet and other large information infrastructures suggest that it is perhaps naïve to think of them as unified socio-technical platforms along which information, events, benevolent and malevolent acts can smoothly propagate (Star & Ruhleder, 1994).

It would be perhaps rewarding to distinguish between unification and interoperability. Without doubt, despite various institutional, social and technical barriers, the Internet contains extended zones of interoperability. This is far from being accidental. Connectivity is the 'essence' of the Internet and interoperability its technical modality (Dreyfus, 2001; Kallinikos, 2006; Zittrain, 2008). It is crucial to understand that, by virtue of being software codes, information-based systems and technologies can potentially be made interoperable even if they are not. No matter how cumbersome it may be, functional compatibility is always a possibility in software code. At the bottom, information-based systems and operations are numerically controlled and for that reason can always be rendered compatible (Kallinikos, 2009a; Manovich, 2001). By way of contrast, there is no way to merge together functionalities, say, of rail and air-traffic technologies. Once transformed into a software code, a product or technology can traverse its previously narrow confines and become an object of communication and exchange along a vast variety of technical and social settings, even though such communication and exchange may require additional technical developments or modifications at higher levels of software. Music and film 'piracy' and cracking of software codes by hackers provide evidence of the standing interoperable possibilities of information-based systems and technologies.

The implications of these developments for the traditional strategies of technological control accomplished through functional simplification and closure are indeed far-reaching. Connectivity and interoperability straightforwardly violate the controlling strategies of functional simplification and closure making the interception of functionalities and the exchange of data and information across information-based systems an essential principle of the new technologies. Needless to say, the understanding of the Internet is a highly complex phenomenon and we cannot do justice to this here. But we can still venture to claim that the diffusion and socio-economic embeddedness of the Internet challenges the traditional forms of technological control and, by extension, the governability of complex sociotechnical systems. In one way or another, the development and diffusion of the Internet takes technology out of the controlled order associated with functional simplification and closure into the messy realm of everyday encounters. This is a major development whose implications for the governance of complex systems are yet to be appreciated (Esposito, 2011; Kallinikos 2009c).

From bounded systems to networks

In this chapter, I have sought to place the understanding of the expanding organizational and economic involvement of information and the diffusion of the Internet against the background of the traditional strategies of technological control. An implicit assumption behind that venture is that current developments can be better appreciated against the background of their similarities and differences to the standard forms whereby technology has been implicated in the construction of predictable worlds and the regulation of social practice.

The influence of information and communication technologies on organization forms and practices has often been assumed rather than analytically examined. New organizational forms, most notably networks, have often been associated with the pervasive character of information technologies that challenge the bounded and concentrated nature of traditional organizations.[7] That association has, however, remained rather vague. It has generally been attributed to the transactional infrastructure of information technologies (i.e., cross-boundary instant interactivity) and the forms of data exchange and communication they enable. The detailed analysis of how information technology reframes and reshuffles the processes, procedures and structures of control in complex systems has never been seriously pursued. Perhaps, as suggested several times in this volume, the spectre of technological reductionism has steered attention away from the detailed study of the organizational implications of technologies. However, even though technologies are not causal forces, they are indispensable means for the construction of social reality.

What I have consequently sought to do in this chapter is to open up that field and examine in some detail the specific ways in which contemporary technologies of information and communication reframe the traditional strategies of technological control that, following Luhmann (1993), I have identified with functional simplification and closure. These developments cannot but have important organizational implications. Functional simplification and closure have been associated with centralized steering practices and management through rigidly segmented, sequentially ordered and hierarchical organizational patterns (Perrow, 1967, 1984; Zuboff, 1988). The normative orientation of traditional technological control is epitomized by the adequate separation of the technical system from the social relations of organizations (Luhmann, 1993). Such a separation has been an essential prerequisite for constructing highly selective and regulated activity corridors along which the social system of organizational roles and positions has been allowed to interact with the secluded order of technical sequences. As I have sought to demonstrate, such a project has always been subject to severe limitations yet it has provided the normative orientation and the grid upon which clearly defined organizational roles and job assignments have been premised and steering mechanisms developed.

The stratified social topology of traditional organization forms, the elaborate systems of formal rules, standard operating procedures, clear-cut job assignments and narrow skill profiles have all been associated with functional simplification and closure. Far from being a causal claim, such a statement attributes to these generic technological strategies an important role in the construction and maintenance of the still-dominant hierarchical organizational practices and forms (Kallinikos, 2004a; Olsen,

---

[7] See, for example, Benkler (2006), Castells (1996, 2000, 2001), DiMaggio (2001) and Knorr-Cetina and Bruegger (2002).

2005). Now the interoperability (actual and potential) of information-based systems and artefacts and the connectivity of the Internet undermine some of the premises upon which functional simplification and closure have been predicated. The strictly regulated activity corridors whereby the social system in organizations was allowed to bear upon the operations of the technical system are partly undermined by the messiness of the Internet and ubiquitous computing. The introduction of new players, some of them uninvited, into the game blurs responsibilities and weakens the patterns of accountability within and across organizations.[8] Boundary-drawing and the regulation of cross-boundary traffic have always been crucial controlling practices that are now partly undermined or reframed by the patterns of connectivity the Internet and ubiquitous computing help establish. Connectivity is, however, on the verge of becoming a worn-out concept. I have thus been at pains to show in this text why this is the case. The software-based constitution of information and communication technologies furnishes the common platform upon which most software-based systems, and the products or services they construct, can be rendered compatible with one another and ultimately interoperable.

The analysis performed here even suggests some important implications for the management of risk that is becoming increasingly a major issue in contemporary society. For all its difficulties, technical risk analysis, based on the calculation of probabilities of unexpected events, safeguarded, and still does so, the operations of technological systems governed by the principles of functional simplification and closure (Rehn, 1998). Probabilities are always inferences about future events, whose validity is based on the availability of data that describes crucial parameters of a well-demarcated system. When such a system is no longer identifiable, technical risk analysis becomes increasingly difficult to apply.

Information and communication technologies and the pervasive character of the Internet thus help establish some preconditions for organizational practices and structural templates alternative to those that have dominated our age. But these possibilities for distributed work patterns, greater individual involvement, flat hierarchies and the likes can be forged into alternative forms of organization only through social struggles. Important technological developments take place against the background of established social relations and a more than a random chance exists that powerful social and

---

[8]The mushrooming literature on mass collaboration (e.g., wikinomics) and the involvement of publics in the making of the products or services they consume are indicative of these trends (see Tapscott & Williams, 2007).

economic elites will seek to shape these developments to accommodate their own interests (Introna & Nissenbaum, 2000; Lessig, 2002; Zittrain, 2008). These struggles, however, cannot be left untouched by the current technological developments as the battle over copyright, open-source software development and peer-to-peer networks show. It is my contention that some of the claims presented in this chapter may assist in clarifying part of the complex picture that has kept emerging for some time now (Kallinikos, Aaltonen & Marton, 2010).

7
Cognitive Foundations of Work: The Workplace as Information

Introduction

The idea that computer-based technology profoundly affects the constitution of contemporary work along cognitive lines must be attributed to Zuboff (1988). She was the first to suggest in a systematic and comprehensive fashion that the diffusion and organizational embeddedness of computer technology tends to transform the physical and social nature of work to an extended encounter with data items of various kinds. In this process, information becomes the predominant medium whereby social and material relations in the workplace are mediated, comprehended and acted upon. A huge and growing electronic text (verbal descriptions, codes and indices, numerical or other relations) engulfs work operations and the social encounters that develop around them. In her own terms, the growing involvement of computer-based technologies *textualizes* social and material relations and thus radically transforms the tangible and social character of work. Several other authors have over the years also delivered scattered observations regarding the cognitive significance of information in restructuring perceptual and action habits at work.[1] However, the theme of the comprehensive cognitive reconstitution of work has still not been pursued systematically. Much cited as it is,[2] Zuboff's work remains, more than two decades after its publication, largely without a companion.

It is not unreasonable to conjecture that Zuboff's moderate influence on management and organization theory may be due to the multidisciplinary character of her investigation. Ironically, the very power of her theoretical

[1] See, for example, Hayles (2002), Sotto (1990, 1996), Weick (1985), Woolgar (2002).
[2] Around 4,500 citations in Google scholar by the time this text was written.

framework, combining insights from various disciplines such as the history of technology, linguistics, cognitive psychology, sociology, philosophy and management, may have impeded the assimilation of her ideas into new research efforts. But it may well be that the technological and social developments that soon after her publication led to the growth of the Internet and the massive diffusion of interoperable information ecologies have tended to obscure the developments she explores in her much-acclaimed book.[3] Other reasons may well include the rigid boundaries of disciplines I have mentioned in the first chapter and the gradual transformation of the credentials of academic appointment and promotion.[4]

The cognitive transformation of the contemporary workplace can be viewed as the outcome of two closely related processes. First, computer technology brings to organizations the abstract conceptual structure and the comprehensive systems of information tokens and codes that sustain software packages. These last are systems of considerable cognitive complexity, framing and structuring their domain of application in terms of data items and the procedures and automated rules by which they are acted upon. Even though complexity is often removed from the interface with which humans interact, elaborate conceptual constructions of this sort cannot but bring into the fields to which they are applied a new working reality that consists of cognitive items (categories and data tokens), and the relationships underlying them.

Secondly, the systematic use of computer-based technology generates an immense output of data and information tokens. Software packages are cognitive machines that classify, order, process, store, retrieve, transfer and control data and information. Once automated information processing is installed, the process tends to become self-propelling. More data demands new computer-based systems for processing information which produce more data and so forth. These developments provide strong evidence of the cognitive orientation of contemporary work and the changing work habits such an orientation by necessity promotes.

It was on similar observations that Zuboff (1988) based her suggestions. Computer-based technology, she claimed, alters the tangible and social nature of work and transforms it literally to *reading*, that is, an encounter with symbol schemes and data items that are supposed to represent surrogate versions of physical and social items and relationships. The

---

[3] See my recent comment in the *Encyclopedia of Software Engineering* dedicated to assessing Zuboff's work more than two decades after its publication (Kallinikos, 2010).
[4] Publications of articles at the expense of long-lasting research pursuits that may turn out risky or unrewarding as publication outputs.

adequate exercise of work increasingly presupposes the cognitive capacity to understand and act upon these elaborate symbolic codifications of work tasks and processes produced by computerization. Cognitive skills are thus increasingly surpassing the bodily and, to a lesser extent, the social skills that characterized the working experience of the industrial age. As defined by Zuboff, cognitive skills mainly involve two major faculties, that is, first, the capacity to connect symbol (data) tokens to the real and tangible world and, secondly, the ability to think in abstract and procedural forms that establish associations and draw inferences from scattered bits of data. In restructuring the infrastructure of work, current technology, she claimed, creates the requirements for new liberating forms of work and social inter-action. However, within the framework of the stratified social topology of organizations, inherited from industrialism, work becomes rather decontex-tualized. The new layers of data produced by computer-based technology and the fixed methods for processing information create novel physical and social distances between organizational employees themselves, and between them and their object of work (Zuboff, 1988, 1996).

The claim that current work is increasingly constituted along cognitive dimensions can, thus, be said to describe the tendency of computer-based technology to redefine the content and forms of work. The massive diffusion of information tokens across contemporary contexts of work removes work practices a further step from the immediacy of things accessed and acted upon through bodily presence. Schematically speaking, it adds another layer of cognitive tokens and techniques between man and the world on those that the organizing practices of modernity have already accumulated in the form of writing and notation of every kind. The distinctive character of this layer is that it consists of impersonal, abstract and comprehensive informa-tion tokens and new largely fixed methods for acting on it, derived largely from formal logic (the software).

The present chapter seeks to re-examine some of these claims in the con-text of a fully computerized dairy plant. The empirical investigation of the tasks and roles assumed by the process operators is described in some detail with the view to show the type of effects the organizational embeddedness of software packages tends to produce. Prior to this, a conceptual framework is outlined that delineates the cognitive issues associated with the recep-tion and understanding of data and information tokens, and the modes of acting on these. Theory and the empirical findings are then juxtaposed and brought to bear upon one another, suggesting a number of emerging themes that describe some of the cognitive work issues associated with the deepen-ing involvement of computer-based technology in social practice.

Theoretical issues: symbol tokens and reality

The encounter with the datafied versions of the world, produced by computer-based technology, is bound up with several subtle cognitive and social issues. A series of challenging research questions remain associated with the perception and understanding of comprehensive systems of codes and symbol schemes occasioned by the diffusion of software packages. Zuboff herself devoted considerable effort to show that computerization creates a distinctive context, where the issues of understanding, relating and acting on symbols and symbol schemes assume crucial importance. In particular, she identified two major groups of related question: 'One involved the relationship of the electronic symbols to a concrete world. The second concerned symbols as a reflection of abstract functions, variables and systemic relationships' (Zuboff, 1988, p. 79).

In some respect, these trends describe the standard division between perception (sensation) and cognition or between tangible reality and abstract concepts. Following a standard linguistic convention, I subsume the analytically distinct processes identified by Zuboff under the labels of *sense* or semantic comprehension and *reference* coinciding with the attribution or association of semantic content to the world 'out there'. The conceptual architecture of a software package, its logic and the conceptual output produced by and through it, require to be semantically comprehended (i.e., the problem of sense), and to be related to real-life situations (i.e., the problem of reference). Therefore, the issue of sense can be said to be associated with the semantic reconstruction and comprehension of the relationships conveyed by a symbol or symbol system – a word, a verbal or numerical statement, a code. The object of sense is the meaning of the symbol system, what it says or conveys. The question of reference, on the other hand, is related to the ability to identify the world correspondence or contextual relevance of the symbol system. The objects of reference are physical objects, states or processes in the physical world (Barthes, 1967; Eco, 1976).[5] If sense asks the question 'what', then reference posits the question what this 'what' is about. The question of reference is always opened by sense (Ricoeur, 1977, p. 217).

Schematically speaking, sense is built up by the meaningful elements conveyed by strings of symbol tokens and strings of such strings. Understanding is drawn towards the interior of a symbol system, as it seeks to comprehend the very relationships whereby the sign system conveys its content.

[5] In analytic philosophy the corresponding terms are intention and extension (e.g., Goodman, 1976).

Reference, on the other hand, involves an opposite exterior movement and demands the 'thingness' or worldly anchoring of the conveyed contents (Borgmann, 1999; Ricoeur, 1977). A sentence, for instance, is sensed through the identification of the syntactic entities and relationships whereby it is composed – that is, subject, verb, object, etc. – and the semantic units it conveys, whereas its understanding is usually further enhanced through the identification of those aspects of the real world it is supposed to represent.[6]

Sense and reference often presuppose one another, as the ability to identify the world correspondences of a sign system or a code enhances the capacity to understand it and *vice versa*. However, the analytic distinction between sense and reference is not simply an intellectual caprice but fulfils several objectives. First, it helps decompose the synthetic totality of the very act of cognizing and thus contribute to its illumination. Distinguishing between sense and reference can trace a mental problem back to its origins, as sense and reference not only enhance but also can contradict or disturb one another.[7] Secondly, the distinction induces one to realize that sense can be associated with mental situations that lack immediate world correspondences. Not only mathematical relations, but even terms such as those of 'effectiveness, 'freedom' or 'interpretation' cannot be pointed or exhibited in any direct way. In addition, larger sequences of token, such as a text or a discourse, create a context replete with meanings and associations that may lack immediate reference. The movement therefore from individual symbol tokens to encompassing symbol outputs establishes a distinct context where reference is suspended, whereas semantic comprehension and interpretation become a complex intellectual endeavour.[8] On the other hand, one and the same object may have two or more meanings, whereas there can be objects or real-life situations that are devoid of an immediate content or meaning, due to uncertainty regarding the interpretive frame to which they belong, that is, an unfamiliar interaction ritual or a strange signal (Burke, 1966, 1981; Ricoeur, 1977).

---

[6] Following a standard convention, I employ the terms 'sign' and 'symbol' as roughly equivalent to designate the use of symbol tokens as carriers of various types of messages and contents. There is an immense literature and controversy on this and other related issues which I here bypass for obvious reasons (see, e.g., Borgmann, 1999; Goodman, 1976; Ricoeur, 1977).

[7] Recall the tense relationship between concepts and facts in the various disciplines.

[8] According to Ricoeur the movement from signs to discourse coincides with the transition from semantics to hermeneutics (Ricoeur, 1977, pp. 216–21). According to him hermeneutics is about the world, that is, it opens the referential question, though not in the same immediate way as individual signs or statements.

Thirdly, the distinction between sense and reference suggests that in the same fashion words exist about other words and numbers about other numbers – that is, concepts of grammar that describe the function of other linguistic terms or mathematical equations that describe arithmetic relations – codes can exist about codes and so forth. Human life in general and software packages in particular are indeed replete with such second- and third-order representations that comprise symbol schemes describing other symbol schemes and relations (Barthes, 1977; Cassirer, 1955; Foucault, 1970). Reference to the physical world is even here suspended and understanding is obtained by relating cognitive items to one another.

The problems of sense and reference are further perplexed as human signification, no matter how strictly literal and closed it may seem, takes places not simply at the plane of denotation but involves, in addition, several connotative meanings. Connotations are metaphoric associations that develop around the denotative core of signifying units and offer a surplus, as it were, of meanings that when inflated may push into the background and even dissolve the underlying denotative symbol or code (Barthes, 1967; Goodman, 1976; Ricouer, 1977). For instance, an organizational chart denotes the functional and hierarchical differentiation as well as the line of command of an organization but may also connote formality, orderliness, rigidity, lack of imagination, etc. Connotations do not stand for an object or state. They relate to the object-world but not in the fashion of denotation – they are metaphoric.

It is important to point out that the delicate character of the processes of cognizing and understanding is inextricably bound up with the fundamental fact that the signification forms of symbol schemes break with the conventions of similarity and proximity as the basic means for signifying. There is no inherent similarity between, say, alphanumeric notation and the contents and real-life situations alphanumeric symbols convey (Barthes, 1967; Goodman, 1978; Leach, 1976). Whereas pictorial representation and indexical signification, to use Pierce's term, rely as a rule on similarity and proximity (e.g., a pointer) as a means for signifying, other symbol schemes, as those of alphabetic, musical or arithmetic notation, represent contrived codes, which do not bear any intrinsic relationship to what they convey or stand for. Forms of signification that are based on similarity and proximity are rich and powerful ways of signifying but, due to their low mobility and context-embeddedness, they remain inextricably tied to 'a here and now'.

In addition, signification based on similarity and proximity achieves often no more than a moderate standardization (Goodman, 1976, 1978), a relation that may inhibit cross-contextual comparisons, as Cline-Cohen (1982) has so admirably shown in her important study on the advent of numeracy in early America. Therefore, forms of signification that are based on similarity and proximity cannot serve the signifying needs of modern man, and the demands of the formal organizations of modernity, operating in an enlarged temporal and spatial frame. Abstract modes of representing and operating address precisely the need of formal organizations to surpass the physical limits of context-embedded action and extend the regulation of human activities beyond 'a here and now' (Kallinikos, 1995, 1996).[9]

Sense and reference are endemic problem situations of contemporary work contexts. They are associated with the current diffusion of formal languages in organizations, and the concomitant proliferation of symbol schemes and codes that do not rely on the signifying conventions of similarity and proximity. However, it would be an awkward gesture to attribute the problems of sense and reference at work to the advent of computer-based technology and the diffusion of software packages alone. Work and social life are inextricably bound up with language, speech and other communicative conventions that make the problem of meaning and understanding endemic to human pursuits.

Indeed, there is ample evidence in organization theory, albeit in a different terminology, that documents various problems of this kind in work settings, that is, difficulties in interpreting cues or signals and associating them with action in ways that promote adaptive learning (see, e.g., Feldman, 1986; March & Olsen, 1989; Weick, 1979b). As a matter of fact, the questions of semantic comprehension and referential attribution of symbol schemes are the outcome of a long historical process of the use of symbol tokens in production and administration (Cooper & Kallinikos, 1996; Hoskin & Macve, 1986). Formal organizations, in particular, are inextricably bound up with decontextualized modes of operations. Comparisons of organizational outcomes across time and space require standardized cognitive devices (e.g., taxonomies, systems of measurement and evaluation) and thus establish modes of operation that break with 'a here and now' (Cline-Cohen, 1982; Hopwood, 1987; Townley, 1994). Bureaucratic organization is itself a system that seeks always to subordinate the specific to the general. Bureaucracy as a social form judges specific occurrences by subsuming them under general categories to which it applies general rules and standardized procedures (Kallinikos, 2006; Perrow, 1986; Weber, 1947).

---

[9] Next chapter explores these relationships in much more detail. See also Lilley, Lightfoot & Amaral (2004).

Decontextualized action and the diffusion of various systems for recording, storing and transmitting information reflect, therefore, a long historical trajectory. At the same time it is important to observe that computerized information systems and software packages create a specific context of signification issues, which owe their distinctive character to the signifying conventions promoted by computer-based technology. Such characteristics include the standardized modes for generating information, the automated rules for processing it, the cognitive complexity of software packages, the comprehensive character of facts and relationships represented by computer-based systems, the extremely high speed and precision for acting on the represented information, the connectivity of various sources of data allowed for by standardized modes of organizing data (databases) that enable the networking of computers, etc. Sense and reference as work problems can thus be said to be accentuated, due to the proliferation of computerized information systems and software packages and the specific cognitive conventions associated with them.

The issues of sense and reference may seem relatively simple in the neat world of analytic thought but are crucially more insidious in the muddled world of real life (Kallinikos, 1995, 1996). The brief exposé above ought to make clear that a copy view of signification that considers signification as an unproblematic, straightforward reflection of an external and pre-existing world, cannot hope to reach far in the ambiguities of real-life situations. The paths of understanding that pass through the dual cognitive tasks of sense and reference are often many, perplexed and criss-crossing, and at other times hardly engraved and distinguishable. Computer-based technology's abstract and decontextualized modes for codifying the production process and other facets of organizational life cannot but accentuate these problems that have been endemic, so to speak, in the formal organizations of modernity (e.g., Cooper & Kallinikos, 1996; Townley, 1994).

The empirical investigation: data tokens and work

The ideas outlined in the preceding section provided me with a loose framework of concepts and concerns that I have sought to further explore in one of the plants of a major dairy cooperative corporation in Scandinavia in which significant computerization has taken place in various waves over the past three decades of the last century. I used the theoretical framework described above as a way of curving out that part of reality which I wished to further explore. Theory in this respect becomes a sensitizing device. While providing an essential means for delimiting an empirical field, theory is too abstract to arrest the observations it helps to produce. It is the exploration of this space that arises from the partial incompatibility of theoretical concepts with empirical observations, the juxtaposition of the general with the particular, and the neat and ordered with the muddle, that yields novel insights (Bateson, 1972; Cassirer, 1955). These epistemological remarks indicate that the overall purpose of the empirical study was no other than to contribute to assessing the relevance, and developing and further specifying the theoretical ideas by allowing empirical observations to enter into a kind of *structured dialogue* with them. Thus used theory becomes an enabling medium that stretches the registering capacity of the researcher and allows the piercing and decomposition of a compact reality. To put it differently, my main objective was to explore the proposition of the cognitive transformation of work and assess the working practices to which the diffusion of information tokens gives rise.

The plant is a dairy of perishables that employs almost 600 employees in three shifts. It takes delivery of approximately 225 million litres of raw milk annually. This is refined and packaged as cream, soured milk, soured cream and milk with a variety of fat contents. The production process is thoroughly computerized and involves the reception of raw milk that is stored in tanks before it passes through several stages of refinement and is then packaged as a variety of dairy products. Since its establishment in 1983, the refinement process has been computerized to almost the same extent as today, however, new production lines were added in 1992–3. Owing to the comprehensive computerization, only a small portion of the work force of the plant is currently employed in the planning and monitoring the reception and refinement of the raw milk.

The study included the investigation of two major groups of work task performed by production operators, namely those of *planning/execution* and *monitoring/control* of the production process. The data collection methods entailed both recorded interviews with operators and supervisors and also site observations of the refinement process in the plant's two computerized control stations. Interviews were semi-structured both by the theoretical concerns outlined above and by a prior reading on the technology of dairy production. Interviews normally proceeded a set of questions concerning the interviewee's background and working duties, and gradually focused on eliciting information about the nature and the character of his work. A total of 27 interviews (all males) were conducted which involved all the process operators and several supervisors. More than half of the interviewees have had experience with less-automated work at four different dairy plants. The interviews allowed therefore for a certain comparison between the work tasks and operations demanded by the plant studied and those of other less-automated factories. Site observations involved participation in several night shifts. Production at night shifts is critical as it determines the availability of the products to be packaged and distributed during the two other day shifts. Both interviews and site observations were carried out separately by the author and a research assistant. All interviews were transcribed and checked by the interviewees.

The bulk of the data was then made of transcribed interviews and field notes taken mainly in the night shifts but also in other occasions. The material was crosschecked by the researchers and triangulated. Data interpretation involved the reading and scanning of this material with the purpose of identifying thematic units. The identification of major and recurrent themes in the empirical material could not be pursued independently of the theoretical concerns that provided a substratum of pre-understandings. Theoretical concepts helped, then, to identify several nodes, that is, important blocks of recurrent concerns, around which clustered the details of the empirical information. The reading process was repeated several times until the number of the initial nodes was reduced to a coherent set of themes related to the empirical setting.

The overall epistemological position outlined above should make clear that the purpose of the case study was not to produce an ethnographic or interpretive account of the empirical context. There was no intention to 'go native' and discover the subjective or shared meanings and associations, which the experience of the process operators created in their minds and bodies. Rather, the objective of the case study was to detach, with the help of concepts, empirical relationships that could be used for understanding wider work transformations, associated with the cognitive orientation of computer-based work. The computerization of the dairy plant was seen as just a particular instance of such wider work transformations (analytic generalization). The empirical investigation was conducted with the view to discover the general in the specific rather than *vice versa*. There was no objective either to judge the very adequacy of the software package – logical, structural or even behavioural. The case study was conducted in order to document modes of action and thought, conceptual habits and procedures related to work underlaid by cognitive items and categories.

Next section reports an edited version of the empirical material that was selected through interviews and site observations. Interviews and field notes have been edited and rewritten to compile a story that conveys major aspects of the production of dairy products and the work duties, procedures and problems facing the process operators. Little wonder that editing and rewriting involves by necessity a form of interpretation. However, the edited story reported below seeks to remain as faithful as possible to the responses of the interviewees and the original field notes.

The technology of dairy production

The production of dairy products involves four major groups of task, that is, (1) the reception and temporary preservation of raw milk, (2) the refinement of the milk into several groups of dairy product, (3) the packaging of the refined products, and (4) the cleaning and disinfecting of the installations.

The second group of tasks, that is, the refinement process, represents the heart of dairy production. The process comprises four distinct steps, that is, pasteurization, separation, homogenization and standardization. With the exception of the stage of separation, the other three stages of the refinement process vary depending on the types of product to be produced. Automation and computerization of dairy production significantly reduced the number of workers employed in the reception and refinement of the products, and considerably limited their physical involvement with the installations where the milk is refined.

Packaging, on the other hand, despite extensive automation, still remains a relatively labour-intensive activity.

In the process bay of the plant studied, the refinement of the milk involves seven treatment lines producing approximately 50 products, many of which represent, nevertheless, variants of major products, for example, milk with variations in fat content. Production is steered from a separate room that forms the production control centre of the plant. Once initiated, the status and progression of production is displayed on panels of bulbs and monitors in the control centre. Several printouts also report incidences in the production process and thus help monitor it. Another control station in the reception bay handles the tasks of milk reception and the cleaning and disinfecting of the installations. The software package provides the means for controlling the quantity of the received milk, channelling it into milk silos where it is preserved at the appropriate temperature before being refined.[10] Quantity is reported both in numerical and analogue form. This last form shows graphically the level of the milk in the silo tanks. The same control station handles the cleaning and disinfecting of the installations. This is technically quite a complex enterprise, since water boiled at high temperature has to pass through all the installations under appropriate pressure.

[10]Quality control involves sensory but mostly laboratory tests.

The upgrading of milk into bulk products in the process bay forms a chained sequence of steps. The operator enters the system, selects the number of the silo and the refinement line, and starts the process by writing on the screen the corresponding command, that is, specifying the product to be produced and connecting the selected silo or silos to the refinement line. The room where the production control centre is located forms the heart of the entire production of perishable dairy products. Production is steered with the aid of two major computers. One of the two machines handles and controls the production of the variants of beverage milk and the other does the same for the production of the various products of sour milk and cream. Both these machines handle the storage of the bulk products, that is, products that have already been refined, in buffer tanks, before they channel them into the corresponding packaging lines. Therefore, the software package in the production control centre provides the means for:

- identifying the quantity of the raw milk and the silo tank where it is kept;
- piping it into the appropriate refinement line;
- specifying the product to be produced. (The specified product determines the refinement pattern, that is, the processes of separation, pasteurization, homogenization and standardization.);
- channelling the bulk products to available buffer tanks, and
- directing the bulk products onto the appropriate packaging lines.

The mechanics of the various processes is steered through electronic sensors and more than 1 000 electronic valves, which connect the seven treatment lines with the three computers in the control rooms. On the shop floor of the process bay, the plant conveys an image of immense complexity. A dense system of pipelines traverses the plant from one end to the other. For the non-initiated the plant forms a hardly supervisable and rather incomprehensible system, but even the process operators made it clear that the totality of the plant is beyond the inspecting capacity of the human senses. When a command is fed into the system, the computer initiates a process by sending electronic signals that pass through so-called process-interface stations and reach out in the installations to control the air pressure in the valves.[11] The air pressure, in turn, regulates a spring, which opens and closes the valves. By this means the electronic signals, initiated by the operator's

[11] Electromechanical devices that transform electronic signals to mechanical impulses and *vice versa*.

commands, steer the passage of milk through the installations. On the other hand, incidences and the progression of the production process are identified with the help of electronic sensors and, passing again through the process- – interface stations, are reported in detail in the production control centre in the form of light signals, monitor codes and printouts. The major steps and variables of the refinement process – that is, the performed functions, boiling time and temperature, air pressure, fat content, etc – are pre-programmed and the process is initiated and executed by the commands process operators feed into the system. Each of the various products obeys its own refinement pattern – that is, different boiling time and temperature, standardization and homogenization, etc – which means the time of refinement of each product differs from three to 24 hours. The process operators always have the option of bypassing the fixed sequence of steps if they think it is necessary or they can reprogram, if they know how, the parameters that determine the refinement pattern of a product. Such moves are, however, risky and they have to be carried out after consultation with experienced operators or the supervisors.

Work tasks and procedures of the process operators

The above description merely gives a wholesale picture of the plant and the production process. Process operators assume a variety of work duties, the majority of which could, however, be grouped into the following four major categories of task:

- *Planning* the various products to be produced, which involves decisions about types of product and quantity, based on information about targeted outputs and available inputs. Planning includes also selection of the refinement line, which involves an estimate of the refinement time of the products under refinement as well as anticipation of the refinement time of the products to be produced. The information based on these decisions is fed into the system which then starts after the appropriate command is given.
- *Monitoring* the refinement process, which involves careful inspection and interpretation of three sources of data reported in the control room, and intervention in the system for restoring occasional deviations and failures.
- *Controlling* the quality of the milk by taking milk from the process bay several times for diverse laboratory testing during the various faces of refinement.
- *Maintaining* the machinery.

The work tasks vary depending on shift and hour. The refinement of the raw milk into bulk products goes on continuously, whereas the cleaning and disinfecting of the installations is dependant on the time each treatment line stands idle once the refinement of a product is completed. The reception of the approximately 700 000 litres daily takes place during 24 hours. The night shift begins with the selection of the types and the specification of the quantity of the product to be produced. Before they feed the commands concerning type and quantity of product into the system, the process operators need to take note of the quantity of the various types of product to be delivered next day, as well as the quantities of the input stock and various types of finished product kept in the refrigerated warehouse. The input stock is checked electronically. With a set of simple instructions the process operator can check the quantity of raw milk and the particular silo in which it is kept. Information about the demand and the availability of finished products is mediated verbally or in written form by the supervisors. Depending on this information, the operator enters the system and performs the following instructions:

- selects the type of product to be produced;
- connects the silo or silos to the refinement line;
- feeds into the corresponding entry the quantity of the product to be produced, and
- starts the process by feeding the appropriate command.

As already indicated, the process is fully automated. Once the necessary data are fed into the system and the start command is given, the process is chained, following its pre-programmed sequence of steps. However, despite or because of the automation of the production process, the majority of the operators interviewed made it clear that the planning of the products to be produced forms a delicate work task. It requires careful inspection of the temporal patterns of refinement of the products to be refined during a shift. The products are selected each time from a population of more than 50 product versions and careful inspection is necessary to take account of different refinement times, as well as the interdependent character of the entire production process. The packaging of products requires available bulk products in buffer tanks and this makes necessary the anticipation of the different refinement times of the various products which, in turn, demands available raw milk in specific silo tanks and so forth. As indicated by the interviewees, local disturbances may rapidly disseminate and have impact on a wide range of activities.

The software package provides the means whereby all these tasks are accomplished. The package is basically an elaborate cognitive map that recaptures the complexity of the installations and the production process (reception, refinement, and preservation of bulk products, selection of packaging line). The conceptual architecture of the package is based on the *functions* and functional steps (e.g., filling, separating, boiling, evacuating, etc.) necessary to accomplish the refinement of the raw milk into bulk products. Functions are tied to particular pieces of *installation* and pertain to *product types* while they exhibit a number of *states* whereby their development is described. Installation pieces, product types, functions and states are mainly coded in forms of discrete symbol tokens, that is, numbers, piece names, functions, but occasionally also in the form of diagrams, coordinate systems and pictures. All cognitive items of the package fall into one of the following four major cognitive blocks or categories as depicted in Table 7:1 below.

The relationships between the cognitive items and blocks of the package are captured, at the human-machine interface, by a long series of simple procedural steps that report the details of the development pattern (e.g., function or state) of the refinement process in the control stations and define the commands whereby the process is steered by the operators. Both the responses of the interviewees and site observations suggest that planning and monitoring the process demands an appreciation of the logic and entities of the software such as software codifications of installation pieces, product types, functions and states as well as the various resulting combinations. Connecting a state with a function, a product type and an installation piece is essential to the tasks of planning and particularly monitoring the process. Incidences in the production, for example, a valve that is not working as it should or problems in filling or evacuating a tank, need be identified rapidly, located and dealt with. For a beginner it may take a good couple of months to get acquainted with the system. Nevertheless, the large number of permutations of installation pieces, functions, states and products indicate that in order to learn the innumerable details and incidences that the production process may occasion may well be a lifelong project. Even the

Table 7.1   Major cognitive categories of the software package

Cognitive categories	Examples
– Installation items and units	– Buffer tanks, refinement lines, valves
– Products and semi-products	– Milk, soured milk, cream
– Functions	– Filling, boiling, evacuating
– States	– Low-level, error, temperature

supervisors indicated they are puzzled by the appearance of codes and print-outs whose meaning or significance they do not fully understand.

An essential requirement for learning effectively how the system works is, according to the majority of process operators, a knowledge of dairy technology, that is, the chemical and mechanical processes necessary to upgrade the milk into bulk products. In order to grasp how the software package works and what it signifies, it is necessary to mentally reconstruct the physical flows and processes regulated by the package. Nevertheless, this requirement is not adequately satisfied in the dairy investigated, since the comprehensive automation of the production process tends to exclude process operators from the shop floor. As a consequence, automation curtails significantly the bodily and contextual involvement of process operators and limits their actions to attending and manipulating the software package and the information it produces. A supervisor described the situation as:

> Those who come from older semi-automated factories know the installations well. Here they just sit and press buttons or look at the bulbs. In order to produce milk here you do not need to know how the milk flows though the installations . . . young operators learn how the system works by following exactly the opposite road: they begin by reading codes and pressing buttons and they build with the passage of time an image of what is going on out in the installations.

The cognitive complexity of monitoring the production process

All the operators' commands are registered in the form of computer print-outs that supply the necessary material for a retrospective analysis and control of the refinement process. Process operators and mostly supervisors indicated that it is important to be able to check and analyse the commands of the operators and their sequential pattern, especially in cases of various failures or mistakes or in cases the where the system reacts by locking itself. Such an examination and analysis of the pattern of commands may provide occasions for organizational learning and end up with changes in the very sequence of commands, or in the pre-programmed variables and parameters of the system.[12] It may also provide, and it occasionally does, the material and the motives for the further training of the process operators into the structure, functions and commands, underlying the software package, and dairy technology in general.

[12] An example of a command is as following: *Tank 07 Evacuation Start.*

Once a treatment line starts, it is monitored by an elaborate system of bulbs that indicate whether the various steps of the production process are running as they should, that is, valves are open or closed and the milk flows through the different stages as programmed and expected. Occasional failures are detected through electronic devices and reported at the production control centre. Sixteen panels with 700 bulbs report the progression and the status of the process. The various bulbs signify this by means of different colours, that is, green (OK), yellow (cleaning) and red (error). Each bulb represents an intersection point in a coordinate system, which is formed by the combination of a piece of the installation with another piece, state or function. For instance, one such point is represented by the intersection of *T08* with *Evacuation* which, in as a green light, means that the milk from the eighth silo tank is under evacuation. Another intersection point in the same panel may be *Pasteurizer 07/T08* which, in as a green light and in combination with the preceding one, conveys the information that the evacuated milk from the eighth silo tank runs into pasteurizer number seven. In this way the bulbs convey information in isolation but mostly through the various combinations they form with other bulbs.

The monitoring system of bulbs essentially decomposes the complex totality of the production process into a large number of discrete steps. Given the complexity of the process it comes as no surprise that the monitoring system, which recounts an essential part of the software package, contains 700 coordinate points. Figure 7.1 shows an image of the cognitive map a panel represents by providing a graphic representation of a portion of one of the 16 panels:

The process is also monitored by two forms of printout that specify occasional failures. One form of printout, called a *process printout*, describes in

T07	T08	T09	T10	T11	T12	T13	T14	
0	0	0	0	0	0	0	0	Error
0	0	0	0	0	0	0	0	Low level
0	0	**0**	**0**	0	0	0	0	Evacuation 1
0	0	0	0	0	**0**	0	0	Evacuation 2
0	0	0	0	0	0	0	0	Pasteurizer 1
0	0	**0**	**0**	0	0	0	0	Pasteurizer 2
0	0	0	0	0	**0**	0	0	Pasteurizer 7 (Sour milk)

Explanation: The bold points show that the bulbs are on, signalling the corresponding state or function, in this case evacuations from silo tanks 9, 10, 12 into pasteurizers 2 and 7.

Figure 7.1 A portion of one of the panels of bulbs showing the state of progression of the production process

codified form the type of failure and locate it in the installations. A typical case of such an error printout looks like *V3154 1→0* which means that the valve number 3154 should be active (1) but it is inactive (0). The number code of the pieces of installation provides an indication of the location of the problem. The same information is supplied by the panel of bulbs whose spatial, geometric organization helps to locate the problem more easily and rapidly. However, neither the system of bulbs nor the written specification of the printouts are capable of locating the problem other than in very aggregate terms, unless the operators have an elaborate representation of the seven lines of the plant in their head, which, as indicated by the operators themselves, is quite often impossible for non-recurrent errors. Thus, starting from the information provided by the system of bulbs and the printouts, the process operators need to consult the detailed design of the installations, as depicted in several engineering drawings. In general, the process printouts are of recurrent character and most operators agree that they are relatively easy to trace and correct. Despite this, situations emerge in which the speci-fication and location of a problem may be proved difficult, especially if a failure occurs towards the end of a shift, after many hours of work.

The second type of printout, which is called a *system printout*, is consider-ably more complex and irregular. This represents an attempt to provide a mechanism that indicates the adequacy of the conceptual and organiza-tional logic of the software package itself. The system reacts on incidences which disturb, for some reason, its own ways to steer the whole process, by delivering an answer (a system printout) as to what such a disturbance could be. In contrast to the process printouts that always indicate a problem in the refinement process, system printouts are attempts by the software package to signal problems in its own capacity, logic and organization to steer and control the refinement process. The extensive character of the definitions, relations, procedures and operations that define the software package itself mean the system printouts are often puzzling and difficult to understand. Many process operators have expressed either a feeling of anxiety or indif-ference (implicit avoidance) towards the system printouts.

The attempt to provide a mechanism, that is, system printouts, that detects how well the software package works involves a new series of cat-egories, codes and definitions (a system of second order) that are brought to bear upon the everyday tasks of process operators (the first order). The documentation of the software package and the installations to which it is related involves 50 manuals of symbol definitions, codes and rela-tionships and functions, a fact that provides an indication of the com-plexity of the situation. The *operator's handbook* contains most symbol definitions, and provides a valuable means for comprehending the nature of the various system printouts. Another group of manuals that is subsumed under the name of *system declaration* provides information of the electronic and physical addresses of various parts of the installation – that is, pumps, valves, process-interface boxes, etc. A system printout of the kind '*OE 07314*' indicates an '*Object Error*' that concerns the representation of the object with the number 07314 and helps to locate it both in the software package and in the installation. All number codes are explained in the manual and their addresses in the software package and the installations are indicated. Another group of manuals that is called *description of functions* contain verbal descriptions of the various functions of the refinement process around which the software package is built, and even the physical mechanisms by which the variables of the refinement process are regulated. A different kind of information is supplied by the so-called *program lists* that provide instructions on how to restart an interrupted process or change, if necessary, the fixed parameters or sequences of the various process steps and their time frames.

The system printouts are collected once every 24 hours. The process engineer, who is in charge of the two control stations, has the task of analysing and explicating them. Apart from the responsibility for the work schedules, the duty of the process engineer is to support the work of process operators by coping with circumstances that surpass the ability of the latter and by providing occasions for learning through hints, suggestions and associations. The process engineer works during daytime and the system printouts are handled mostly retrospectively and often in close connection and consultation with the supplier of the software package. During the other two shifts, when the process engineer is not present, the process operators are assumed to be able to take care of the system printouts and initiate corrective action themselves, if they judge it necessary.

Both, the responses of the overwhelming majority of the interviewees and sight observations suggest that coping with the system printouts is associated with feelings of distress and anxiety. As a rule, the process operators do not and cannot know in advance what all these various system printouts mean and what consequences they may have for the refinement process. The language of the system printouts is technical. It aims mostly at providing information to the process engineer and the supplier of the software package on how the system works. Most of this information has to be analysed systematically by specialized staff of the company and the supplier of the system (hardware and software), to initiate changes in the parameters and procedures of the system when necessary. Only a few operators with considerable knowledge in programming or with an inclination for abstract, procedural thinking can cope reasonably well with the system printouts.

The operators in charge of the afternoon and night shifts must make a decision as to whether a system printout can be put aside and await analysis the next day or be dealt with immediately. Therefore, the operators are supposed to be able to undertake searches in the extensive written documentation of the software package that is kept inside the production control centre. The first task, then, when facing a system printout, is to be able to decide whether the failure it indicates is as serious as to require immediate intervention or whether it is not urgent and, therefore, can be left to be taken care of by the process engineer or the supplier of the package the next day. If a system printout is interpreted as indicating a serious failure, the process operators in charge must make up their minds as to whether they can themselves cope with the situation or whether they need to alarm the system and call for emergency service assistance. It takes a great deal of experience to be able to make these decisions in a reasonably short period of time. It comes, then, as no surprise that the process of decoding system printouts is often associated with problem-oriented oral exchanges and joint problem-solving. By these means, operators use one another's experience and cross-validate their views, as they seek to produce a reasonable response to the situation confronting them.

The attitude of the process operators *vis-à-vis* the system printouts and also *vis-à-vis* the steering of the refinement process by means of the software package in general is revealing with respect to the sort of feelings and predispositions associated with computer-controlled production. Most of the operators, especially the older ones, feel that the lack of proximity to the physical flows and the installations represent a major issue that brings several negative consequences. First, it deprives them the ability to perceive the actual production process and locate occasional failures or problems during the refinement. They have to mentally reproduce these situations by relying on the cues and the codes of the system alone. Secondly, they claim that the resulting vague picture they have in their minds of the actual production process and the physical layout of this particular plant impedes the adequate understanding of the various flows, and makes them feel insecure about what is going on in the plant. Furthermore, most process operators find the software package and the language of its documentation difficult to comprehend. The 50 manuals that comprise the documentation of the software package and the installations are classified in groups that facilitate inspection, procedural reasoning and effective use, but classification does not eliminate the problems facing the process operators. It is a generally agreed upon fact in the production control centre that the descriptions and instructions found in the documentation of the software package and the installations are difficult to comprehend or they are, as they say, written in the 'wrong' way. While recognizing the technical superiority of the plant thus controlled and organized, most operators, with prior experience in semi-automated plants, decry the loss of the opportunity of physical acquaintance with the installations. They consider the lack of knowledge of the tangible reality of the plant as a severe limitation.

The ability to use the existing documentation and managing to navigate the huge number of pages, filled with codified information and elliptic verbal statements, improves with the accruing experiential knowledge that the acquaintance with the system confers. Experienced operators are generally believed to be more capable in coping with the emerging situations that system printouts indicate. But the system also demands abstract faculties and these do not need to be associated with working experience in a linear fashion. Furthermore, behavioural predispositions as curiosity, patience and stress tolerance are important worker characteristics. In stressful conditions it may prove difficult to find a matching description of a given problem in an emergency.

In sum, the work of the process operators consists of planning, running and monitoring the production and refinement processes at a distance. Their physical involvement is considerably limited. In the production control centre, in particular, the process operators' contacts with the physical means of production, and the very transformation of material flows, are mediated, almost exclusively, through the fingerboard/monitor, the conceptual organization of the software package and by a complex system of bulbs that codify the flow of the production process. The refinement process continues through all three shifts, but this production control centre is thus insulated so as to be deprived from the various incidences that mark the passage of time, that is, sunlight and season. The relatively few bodily and physical actions of the process operators occur when they exit from this neutralized work environment to maintain the installation pieces and take sample tests of the quality of the products under refinement. In less computerized, semi-automated factories many of these operations were performed by human labour with the help of mechanical and electronic means located at the shop floor, usually in the proximity of the corresponding installation pieces. A process operator commented on the work environment of the production control centre as follows:

> From those that pass by here, there are certainly many that believe that we do not do anything but sit and look at the bulbs. But here we do work

with the head instead. It is hard to work with the head and boring to stay in front of the panels and the monitors the whole day.

Emerging themes

The planning and monitoring of the production process by means of software shows that the effective exercise of the process operators' work tasks involves understanding and acting upon a complex structure of quasi-analogue but mostly digital representations. Representations of this kind segment the composite totality of the production process into small, supervisable steps, the relationships of which are captured in terms of simple causal or sequential connections. They thus provide a mirror image of the production process, framed in terms of symbol schemes and combinations, and signalling systems. It is this elaborate system of cognitive pieces and relationships, symbol schemes and codes that becomes the fundamental means for carrying out the tasks and operations that define the work of process operators.

The pronounced cognitive orientation of process operators' work is reflected, rather unambiguously, on the nature of the tasks performed by them most of the time. It is only natural that in the work environment of the control stations and, more specifically, in the production control centre physical involvement and social encounters are kept at a minimum. As the tangible character of production is receding into the background, the cognitive items, structures and relationships of the software package become the only means for process operators to reach out to the world and bring effects on it. Figuratively speaking, the software becomes their arm whereby they grasp the things 'out there'. Paying attention to pre-structured systems of signals and symbol schemes, understanding and relating them to the world, drawing inferences and providing associations, these seem to be the elements that make up the growing cognitive universe that becomes their work.

However, even though the present study offers an empirical illustration of the postulated cognitive orientation of work, these ideas are not unknown in social science at large and the more delimited field of workplace and organization studies. The advent and diffusion of various systems and practices for storing, ordering and indexing data and information, and the proliferation of elaborate but often quasi-fixed methods for making projections and drawing inferences – that is, specialized notation as accounting, writing in general, statistical methods of inference, etc. – are constitutive characteristics of the formal organizations in modernity (see, e.g., Cooper,

1989; Cooper & Kallinikos, 1996). Various authors of differing disciplinary affiliations have over the years delivered similar observations to those advanced above.[13] What, then, does the present study contribute? As with most studies, the present one does not develop apart from other investigations. It draws on their insights, critically approaches some of them, ponders and reframes others to explore clusters of ideas that appear to be associated with the cognitive constitution of work. Here are some emerging themes that it offers as novel insights.

Issues of referential attribution

As it is revealed by the power of examples in illustrating abstract ideas, reference to reality is essential to understanding (Cassirer, 1955) even though, as Ricouer (1977) notes, the problem of reference is opened by sense as logically prior to reference. The tangible and contextual character of reality conveys evidence of the understandability of abstract relations, which are thereby anchored to reality. The significance of the referential world in human understanding and the cognitive issues associated with reference are in the present study shown in the very design of the signalling system for monitoring production. Having separated the mechanics of the production from the immediate perception of the process operators, the designers of the plant have attempted to compensate for the lack of referential reality by constructing an elaborate signalling system for monitoring production that facilitates referential attribution. Such a system achieves an economy of perception through the arrangement of bulbs in a geometric fashion that makes them easy to perceive and inspect. As shown in Figure 7.1, the signalling system for monitoring the production process restores a sense of cognitive orientation. Through clear and schematic correspondences between symbol token and referent, it provides a relatively unambiguous means for tracking the references of the reported information, and a sort of a substitute for the feeling of the lost tangibility and contextuality of referential objects and processes.

In this regard, the centrality of the issues associated with the referential attribution of software codes or messages can be said to show most conspicuously in the geometric arrangement of the system of the bulbs. Such a spatial distribution of the reported information is built, wittingly

[13]See, for example, Göranzon (1992), Knorr-Cetina and Bruegger (2002), Miller and O'Leary (1987), Sotto (1990), Walsham (1993), Weick (1985), Woolgar (2002), and, of course, Zuboff (1988).

or unwittingly, on the presupposition that reference is or can become a problem, under abstract and decontextualized conditions of work. The major concern of the spatial design of the signalling system is to facilitate the inspection and control of the production process. In providing a form of unambiguous information, it helps the process operators locate relatively easily what is going on in a complex technological landscape of numerable installation pieces, and electromechanical and chemical processes. The bulbs are arranged to recapture the totality of the production process, through the decomposition and elaborate segmentation of its various steps, which are then geometrically represented as points in coordinate systems.[14] A sort of a structural resemblance is thus established between the bulbs (symbol tokens) and the absent reality of the refinement process (reference).

Furthermore, the geometric arrangement of the signalling system contains an indication of temporal patterns. The static picture of intersection points is complemented by the arrangement of lamps in ways that recapture the fixed technological progression of the production steps. By employing the institutional logic of writing, the points (bulbs) in each panel follow a serial and a vertical pattern of development from left to right and from top to bottom. The 16 panels are themselves arranged in a development pattern from left to right that captures the more comprehensive steps of the technological progression chain. The panel that represents the input stock of raw milk is located on the left side. The panels that recapture the steps of pasteurization, separation, homogenization and standardization are immediately to the right of it and the panels that represent the buffer tanks with the various types of refined bulk milk are on the right of the preceding ones. At the end of right side of the control station are the panels that report the process whereby the products in buffer tanks are channelled into the various packaging lines. In this way the logic of the adjacent relations of the physical entities is reintroduced into the system. In addition to the geometric arrangement of the system of bulbs and panels, the feeling of referential reality is enhanced by almost ten pictorial representations supplied by the computer monitors. The pictures portray the levels and quantities of the various products at different stages.

Thus, through the spatial-geometric arrangement of the signalling system for monitoring production and the monitor pictures, the process operators are able to obtain a comparatively quick, unambiguous and fair

---

[14]In more recent dairy technologies, monitor diagrams that follow, by and large, the same arrangement principles and configuration patterns have replaced the system of bulbs.

inspection of the status and the progression of the various treatment lines that constitute the totality of the refinement process. The sophistication and the relative complexity of this system of surveillance emerges on the background of its capability to monitor seven production lines, the numerable products of which obey widely different temporal and refinement patterns that are recaptured by a population of 700 bulbs. As indicated above, the signalling system can be said to achieve an economy of perception and referential attribution.

On the basis of these observations, it could be claimed that the geometrical representations of the panels of bulbs provide evidence of the importance attributed to reference in work environments that no longer involve bodily and context-embedded work. Lacking the multiple cues provided by immediate perception, humans must be supplied with relatively unambiguous signs that help them establish associations and cause–effect relationships, on the basis of which they can undertake meaningful action. The panels of bulbs provide just such simple model of associations, consisting of two variables or factors that report states of functions in the production process. They thus help recall the tangibility of the plant and locate the installation piece and the process referred to. In its relative simplicity, the monitoring of the production through the geometrical arrangement of the points in the panels shows essential characteristics of work cognitivization: in the place of the tangibility and holistic perception of the objects and processes of context-embedded work appears an extensive series of coded versions of these. Proximity and bodily involvement are transformed to discontinuous codifications.

The issue of referential attribution in the dairy is also addressed by the process printouts. The careful specification of the location of a problem this kind of printout produces also represents evidence of the importance of the process of referential attribution in decontextualized work settings. Convincing as it may be in providing an overall orientation, the geometric arrangement of the bulbs and the panels remains imprecise as far as detailed incidences or disturbances in the mechanics of the production process are concerned. In a relatively simple, precise and straightforward fashion, the process printouts come to complement the system of bulbs, by indicating through numerical descriptions the installation item concerned and through binary coding (right–wrong, active–inactive) the state to which it finds itself. However, due to the huge size of the factory and the complexity of the installations, the process printouts may fail to provide a clear response as to what they stand for. After all, numerical description requires contextualization in order to become meaningful. Therefore, a third stage in the information search involves the consultation of the much more detailed description of the plant drawings, in the hope that the problem can be located in this way.

It could therefore be claimed that the monitoring of the production process involves an extensive information-seeking, code-interpreting process, with a view to connecting the software codifications to the absent reality, developing beyond the walls of control stations. The design of the production control centre, and the nature and types of sign produced by the automated system aim at alleviating major problems of referential attribution. Despite all these rather sophisticated substitutes for the referential reality of immediate perception, the lack of proximity to the installations still haunts many process operators, especially the older ones. Cognitive habits established during a lifetime do not change easily. The vicarious representations of the software package fail to restore the confidence that referential reality is capable of providing to people accustomed to context-embedded work, based not just on the reasoning and distancing capacity of the eye but on sensory-motor manipulation of tangible things (Sotto, 1990; Zuboff, 1988). One process operator summarized the situation as follows:

> In less-automated factories we worked out at the shop floor. We knew how the machines should sound and identified problems very rapidly ... each pump had its own distinctive sound. Here you cannot hear anything unless a very serious failure threatens the plant.

The lack of proximity to the referential world gives rise to certain cognitive paradoxes that I return to, after the treatment of the issues, which are associated with the semantic comprehension of the items and relationships conveyed by the software package.

Semantic comprehensibility and associations

Sense and meaning are intrinsic to human cognition. Comprehensibility always proceeds from cues or symbol tokens, that is, the syntactic level of signification, to the contents or meanings conveyed by tokens, that is, the semantic level. It presupposes the ability to identify semantic units and trace them along their semantic paths. The production of sense presupposes the ability to link, reshuffle and recombine semantic units and thus provide associations and draw inferences that are not straightforwardly evident at the first level of meaning. Insofar as the making of sense presupposes the decoupling of the faculty of comprehensibility from referential attribution, sense is bound up to lead to more or less abstract and context-free forms of reasoning.

The analysis of the empirical data on the tasks of process operators suggests that semantic associations take place at different levels, with varying degree of complexity. The first encounter at the human-computer interface conveys the impression of a relatively smooth and undisturbed interaction. One or other question may occur in the control rooms but it is usually dealt with without significant complications. It is evident that the codified representations of the software package alter the conditions of work by providing an elaborate system of cognitive items and relationships, but they do so in a fashion that *prima facie* does not seem problematic.

Another picture emerges, however, when one considers the depth of the software package and the problems associated with understanding and coping with the system printouts. The distinctive character of the problem of semantic comprehension, in this case, seems to be closely associated with the conceptual architecture of the software package. Rather than being a one-level cognitive structure, the software package for planning and monitoring the production process forms a hierarchical or multilayered and self-referential system of definitions and relationships, composed by successive and increasingly inclusive orders of representations. The system printouts and the system documentation to which they are tied make clear that the understanding of codes, definitions and statements at one level of the package are often semantically captured by recourse to more inclusive statements and definitions.

As soon as the system fails, for some reason, to steer and monitor production the way it should, a new abstract landscape of considerable cognitive complexity begins to loom in front of the eyes of process operators. They know and have made it clear in various ways that in order to deal with serious system disturbances it is necessary to be capable of addressing this second- and third-level software representations that are pre-programmed attempts of the system to control or signify itself. Therefore, understanding and coping with the circumstances signified by the system printouts entail a movement towards the interior, as it were, of the software package, rather than a movement towards referential reality. It is as if the process operators have to turn their backs on the physical production process and devote themselves instead to the task of examining the very structure of signs, codes and symbol schemes whereby physical relationships are mediated and regulated. The immediate object of work is not the physical production itself but the mechanisms of steering and controlling it at a distance. Whereas the issue of reference involves the construction of correspondences between sign and referent, the system printouts make clear that the codifications of the software package do not represent a mirror image of the material and technological constitution of the work processes. Rather, they seem to produce a fragmented, multilayered system of signs and codes that resembles more, to use a metaphor, several cubist paintings superimposed one upon another than a realist, representational painting.

In addition to the multilayered organization of software packages and the cognitive issues associated with it, the empirical data suggests that semantic comprehension is further impaired by the logical roots of conceptual and software engineering. The established conventions of electronic codification and programming break with the signifying means of similarity and proximity, and other intuitive yet vital modes of human understanding, including metaphor, abductive associations, intermodal communication, etc. (Boland, 1987; Eco, 1976; Weick, 1985). The logical make-up of the software package is forcefully revealed by the comments of most process operators and the dominant view in the control rooms that the system documentation is written in the 'wrong' way. Both the design of the installations and the software package are the cognitive output of a conceptual and experiential context, that is, engineering and programming, that differs essentially from that of the process operators and traditional forms of work involvement in general.

The problems of sense associated with the multilayered and self-referential conceptual organization of the software package can perhaps be exemplified by means of the conceptual requirements facing the work of the dictionary- or lexicon-maker.[15] Having, by the nature of the task, been deprived of the possibility of using the reality of tangible things, the dictionary-maker has no other means of explaining the entries of the dictionary but other entries which, in turn, cannot be explained unless by means of other entries, and so on.[16] Software packages can be said to exhibit the same problematic. The experience of process operators with the system printouts shows that these self-pondering, auto-referential operations are prone to create a context of infinite regress, a vortex, as it were, of increasingly abstract representations that puts their sense making capacity under a hard test. As one process operator forcefully commented:

> Quite often I have the feeling that what is asked from us is not to work but to understand how the software package regulates production, in order

---

[15] The dictionary is, of course, multilayered only in the indirect fashion of words and concepts exhibiting various degrees of abstraction and generality, for example, the concept of the 'apple tree' can be subsumed under the more general concept of 'tree'. Software packages usually exhibit a depth which dictionaries lack.
[16] Exemplifying pictures can only be used marginally.

to be able to intervene in few cases or in other cases the system fails ... to understand the system one has to understand its logic, to have an image of how it is built and functions.

The empirical material even suggests a series of additional and important questions. The problems of process operators in understanding the structure and the conceptual output of the software package appear to be associated with the meaning of elaborate cognitive products in their entirety. If signifying products were made up of individual units arranged in adjacent or even hierarchical patterns then human signification would have been simple but also impoverished. Elaborate cognitive systems, and the products which are produced through them cannot be understood by recourse to the individual units comprising them, but entail a new level of understanding that must be sought in their composite totality (Borgmann, 1999). The transition from individual signs to more encompassing sign systems occasions the central problem of interpretation which differs from sheer semantic comprehension that is thus seen to apply to simpler or relatively separate cognitive or signifying blocks (Ricoeur, 1977).

Theories of signification often distinguish between primary signs, sentences and discourses. Interpretation evolves in the domain of discourse whereas semantic comprehension applies to signs and sentences. No matter whether one accepts Ricoeur's suggestions or not, software packages could be viewed as occasioning a problem of understanding which, *mutatis mutandis*, recounts that of discourse. A discourse taken as a whole may lack immediate reference but is often associated with several meanings and morals, which are interwoven in its very texture. In a similar fashion, it could be claimed that it is the software package as a whole and also technology's particular forms of embodying human agency, by means of its painstakingly automated operations, which must be grasped to occasion a wider understanding of particular instances or codes. No matter how indirectly, contemporary work seems to be inescapably exposed to these situations, which inhere in the ways work is currently conceived and instrumented. The next chapter takes us on a tour across history that shows in the evocative prose of fiction this to be intrinsic to modern life.

The experiences of the process operators recorded in this study could be associated with these wider cognitive demands, which the understanding of software packages in their entirety seems to occasion. On the one hand, process operators recognize the superiority of the software package in planning and monitoring the production process. The majority of them agree that the package controls effectively most of the circumstances surrounding the reception and refinement of the milk. As a consequence, it makes easier for them to achieve an inspection of the installations and the whole process that would otherwise have been difficult. On the other hand, they seem to lose sight of the purpose of the package and fail to accept that the use of computer technology implies the transition to sort of order that regulates not simply the machinery but even automates human agency. In so doing technology imposes specific demands on human behaviour, the particular details of which most process operators have difficulties to connect with the overall purpose of the software package and the automation it implies. There is little doubt that the difficulties in understanding the overall purpose of the automation are closely associated with the mentioned multilayered and logical make-up of the software package.

Superstitious associations

The perplexing character of the problem of sense in contemporary work settings may convey the idea that semantic comprehension is more crucial than that of referential attribution. From a certain point of view this is true. Being logically prior to reference, sense defines a wider territory of questions. On the other hand, referential reality assumes a sort of ontological primacy in human cognition, a primacy that is good not to lose sight of. After all, sense and reference are inescapably connected with one another. Indeed, the loss of semantic comprehension may often be accompanied by the inability to find the referential objects of a codified message, whereas referential reality may promote comprehensibility.

The interdependent character of sense and reference is associated with several other interesting themes that are the outcome of the different roads to learning and understanding that sense and reference represent. The empirical observations here, as recaptured by the reactions and comments of process operators, when they face issues of abstract reasoning and semantic comprehensibility, seem to suggest that reference can be substituted for sense. When facing the decoding of the system printouts, the majority of the process operators lament the distance separating them from the installations, where they think 'true' things are happening. The difficulties in understanding the manuals comprising the plant's documentation and the software package are mistakenly attributed to the lack of referential reality. They would prefer to identify and cope with the problem in its physical setting. Referential attribution alone cannot, however, resolve the problem of sense but in marginal ways. To substitute reference for sense is not an unusual human reaction and it seems not be unconnected with the asserted ontological primacy of perception. However, such a reaction misconstrues the problem at hand. Once lost in an unknown terrain, the map is as a rule, more useful than random, instinctual explorations of the territory. It is also obvious that the semantic issues associated with the multilayered character and the depth of software packages, exemplified in this case by the problems of understanding and dealing with the system printouts, cannot be addressed by the kind of knowledge created by proximity to installations, particularly not in highly automated and interdependent systems of production, as the one reported in this chapter.

The tendency to substitute reference for sense is not unrelated to the current organization of work and the forms of learning such an organization seems to encourage. As indicated by the comments of the supervisor earlier in the description of the case, automation and computerization tend to promote a form of learning that proceeds from sense to reference or, to use another terminology, from the context-free and general to the contextual and particular. Substituting, then, reference for sense might be a reaction that, wittingly or unwittingly, seeks to counterbalance the excessive abstractions of the post-industrial work and the troubles they seem to engender for the average worker (March & Olsen, 1976, 1989; Zuboff, 1988).

The opposite response, that is, to substitute sense for reference, amounts to avoiding confronting a situation by replacing encounters with the object-world, either with disembodied meditations or with the random or aimless exploration of the cognitive items of a package. Such a reaction has been exceptional at the control rooms. There has been, however, some indication suggesting that the complexity of the production process and the installations may produce such a reaction. Young process operators particularly with less experience in bodily, contextual work and a vague picture of the mechanics of the production process seem more prone to substitute sense for reference than older process operators. An older process operator with experience in less automated factories summarized the situation as follows:

People are different, some prefer to go out in the installations and check what is going on. But there are others who refuse to move, they just sit down and open the manuals one after the other, looking for a solution to the problem. It is not easy to say which method is best. Certainly, you cannot identify what is wrong many times by just rushing out in the installations.

The issues raised by exchanging sense and reference are not unrelated to earlier works on decision-making and thinking, under equivocal conditions that favour the construction of spurious associations, what March and Olsen (1976) have referred to as superstitious learning and learning under ambiguity (see, also, Feldman, 1986; Weick, 1979). It would seem that under complex and ambiguous conditions, reference may be substituted for sense and *vice versa*, as organizational members seek by all means to produce what they feel can be reasonable and comprehensible accounts of the situation confronting them. In other words, there can be cases in which the lack of semantic comprehension or interpretation of a symbol scheme or code ends up with the firm embrace of the convincing tangibility and contextuality of the referential world. On the other hand, there may be situations in which the semantic comprehension of a symbol scheme is employed, and perhaps elaborated, as a means for supplementing the reference deficit of a recalcitrant and confusing reality. Both these responses are deliberately used by artists as a means for reconstructing the conventions, underlying perception and understanding (Barthes, 1977; Bateson, 1972) and may have positive effects in experimenting with alternative courses of action in organizations (Kallinikos, 1996; March & Olsen, 1976).[17] More than often, however, the confusion of sense and reference tends to produce a skew understanding of the confronted situation (Bateson, 1972). These could be interesting questions to address in future research.

Concluding remarks

This study suggests that computer-based technology and software packages can be conceived as cognitive systems, which impose their order on work organizations, in the form of elaborate conceptual categories, items and relationships and fixed methods and procedures for processing storing and acting on data and information. The semantic comprehension of the cognitive items and relationships of software packages and their relation to the referential world become, thereby, central problems of contemporary work organizations. The semantic comprehension of digital data tokens involves a set of issues, which are inescapably connected with the multilayered, elaborate, self-referential, and logic-based constitution of software packages. Reference, on the other hand, demands the appreciation of what software codifications are supposed to stand for, how they relate to the referential

---

[17] See March's *Technology of Foolishness* contained in March and Olsen (1976) and Kallinikos's chapter *Tools, Toys and Metaphors* in Kallinikos (1996).

world, a task which no matter how difficult it may happen to be, appears more tractable. It is reasonable to conjecture that the cognitive demands which sense and reference put upon organizational members may differ, depending on the architecture of the package, the nature of the tasks to be monitored and other circumstances recounting the distinctive conditions of particular work organizations.

Here we touch certain of the limitations that underly the present study. No matter how important, the computerization of process industry covers only a small fraction of the entire gamut of work issues associated with the diffusion and organizational embeddedness of information technology. It is also reasonable to infer that the predictability of industrial production lends itself more easily to automation and its control and monitoring at a distance. The project of constructing a cognitive-linguistic theory of work in the age of information needs, therefore, to pass through both the investigation of other empirical contexts and even involve the more successful integration of the relevant available literature. It also needs to search for, in theory and practice, 'ways of worldmaking'–to use Goodman's (1978) suggestive title and insights– that is, how people associate and infer, tinker and improvise, project, delete, compose and decompose, perspectivize, order and weigh, deny and falsify different cognitive items and relationships to arrive at reasonably sensible worlds. The present study merely offered a sketch of how such a theory might look like and some hindsight on how to proceed with it.

It is, however, indicative of the relevance of the observations put forth in this chapter that similar problems abound and in a sense get intensified by the diffusion of the Internet and the penetration of every walk of life by information-based artefacts (Morville, 2005). In a recent edition of *Wired* its editor Chris Anderson traces similar problems as the outcome of what can be called 'datafication of life', that is the mediation of most aspects of contemporary living by data produced and processed by powerful computer technologies.[18] I reflect on these wider issues in the last chapter.

---

[18]July 2008. See also *The Economist*, 27 February–5 March 2010.

8
Information Tokens and Reality: A Parable of the Internet

Information tokens and the Internet

In the preceding chapter I have been at pains to demonstrate to some degree of detail the manner in which the deepening involvement of information technologies in the workplace profoundly affects the nature of work and how it is exercised. The analysis has shown a wide range of tasks and operations that have traditionally been entangled in a considerably mechanized yet tangible production process to be increasingly transformed into an encounter with information tokens that codify the realities of production and steer and control its course. Reality is increasingly carried on the shoulders of information tokens and the rules (software) that govern their generation and dissemination.

Rather than being an isolated phenomenon, the transformation of the workplace along these lines represents an instance of wider developments that recount a long journey of human distancing from immediate contexts through the invention and deployment of a range of symbol systems and schemes (Benedikt, 1991; Cassirer, 1955). Human language itself has always carried a tense relationship to reality, being both its inseparable companion and, at the same time, its adversary, an *other*, as it were (Flusser, 2000, 2002). Through language and the vast cognitive and communicative space it opens, humans have in the course of civilization invented a variety of representing conventions, specialized systems of writing and notation that have been deployed to represent, mediate, construct and control the world (Borgmann, 1999; Wertsch, 1991).[1] The multivalent involvement of such systems in human affairs has

---

[1] Numbers are always about something; in other words, numbers presuppose a semantics (the meaning of aboutness), which is mediated by language (see Frege, 1950).

brought about the description of the world along the categories of these systems and accordingly eroded immediacy to reality and context-embedded forms of human interaction in a long process of historical evolution.

It is little wonder then that these developments represent an uneven evolutionary trajectory (see Cassirer, 1955; Goody, 1986; Ong, 1982). The aggregate and historical perspective from which I view them here indicates no more than a general trend that is unevenly refracted across the various areas that constitute the institutional landscape of human societies. It would perhaps be possible to claim that scale and institutional complexity are historically correlated (in positive ways) with the invention and deployment of symbol systems and schemes such as accounting and budgeting, finance, and various systems of cataloguing and indexing. Indeed, Beniger (1986) tracks the emergence of the information society to the administrative techniques deployed to control the huge productive forces that industrial capitalism set in motion. A variety of techniques, systems of measurement and auditing as well as a range of writing skills and occupations grew out of the effort to effectively monitor the production and distribution of mass products and services across the extended territories of national and international markets.

These observations suggest that most symbol systems and schemes, including those of art (such as music notation), are the inevitable accompaniment of human pursuits. They arise out of the efforts of individuals and groups to manage the world and render it meaningful through the erection of stable communicative structures of recognition and control. Similarly to the human language from which they ultimately derive, most of the non-verbal symbol systems and schemes carry a subtle and contradictory relationship to the reality to which they relate (Flusser, 2002). On the one hand, they untangle its composite and often opaque nature and, in so doing, allow the cognitive inventions of the human mind to describe, understand and control it. There should be no doubt that this results in a richer understanding of the world. On the other hand, as Cassirer (1955) claimed more than half a century ago, all these symbols systems and schemes, including those of verbal language, carry the 'curse of mediacy', the unavoidable distancing or separation from the reality they address (Borgmann, 1999). Mediation never comes alone but carries a great train made of misperceptions, emulations, fabrications, illusions and lies (Bateson, 1972; Nardi & Kow, 2010).

In an interesting and innovative way, these issues are currently re-emerging with ample force in the information affluence of contemporary world and the saturation of most walks of contemporary living by data of every sort (Anderson, 2008; Kallinikos, 2009a, 2009b). In a sense, the Internet could be seen as the epitome of the longstanding evolution whereby symbol tokens reclaim reality. From a technical point of view, the Internet is no more than the invention of protocols (standards) that allow the transference of data from one source to another. But from the perspective I advocate in this volume, the Internet is a comprehensive, albeit fragmented, cognitive/communicative grid that makes symbol (data) tokens as pervasive as central elements in mediating reality.

Through and by means of the Internet, a variety of cultural conventions and systems of representing reality converge in a vast interoperable platform that thus becomes the cognitive and communicative grid on the basis of which reality is perceived and acted upon. Thus seen, the Internet carries layers upon layers of symbol tokens of various breeds and kinds (e.g., text, image or sound, databases and multiplayer games, information services of all kinds) that separate contemporary humans from the world at the same time as they offer the technical modalities for (re)connecting to the world and to one another. These trends have undeniably been observed in the literature but the issues they raise are both proliferating and puzzling (Kallinikos, Aaltonen & Marton, 2010).[2]

The conception of the Internet as a vast cognitive platform by means of which reality is reclaimed also contrasts with the understanding of the Internet as a liberating communicative medium that allows one-to-one interaction to bypass the constraints of centrally-controlled, one-to-many communications associated with the techno-institutional assemblage of mass media. This is a recurring theme in the current discourses of media and the Internet (Benkler, 2006; Bolter & Gruzin, 2002; Jenkins, 2006). According to this view, the Internet is made possible through the end-to-end architecture of computing machines. The key to this architecture is the central role which individual computing machines (and users) play and the leeway this provides for individual freedom and creativity as fat, intermediate layers of institutionally controlled information get weakened and end-users are empowered (Benkler, 2006; Zittrain, 2008). Fragmentation, creativity and individualization that the current end-to-end architecture of the Internet affords thus contrast with the homogenizing tendencies which a comprehensive cognitive/communicative platform of the kind I describe here may seem to promote.

However, though seemingly at cross-purposes, the two portraits of the Internet presuppose and, in some way, reinforce one another. The flexible

[2] See, for example, Benedikt (1991), Bolter and Gruzin (2002), Borgmann (1999, 2010), Castells (1996), Dreyfus (2001), Hayles (1999, 2005, 2006) and Zuboff (1988).

interaction and communication patterns that end-to-end computer architectures promote are descriptions of social forms (e.g., Wikipedia, open
source) and not of the cognitive and communicative material and media
by which such forms are sustained. It is a key attribute of the Internet that
the stuff of the social forms it allows to emerge is information tokens produced and disseminated technologically. Such a condition has far-reaching
implications for the nature of the social bonds thus constructed as well as
the forms and conventions through which information tokens are used to
mediate reality. Distance communication cannot occur unless the tokens
whereby communicative messages are conveyed are de-anchored from its
fixity to people and things (Borgmann, 1999; Kallinikos, 1996). About these
developments, Benkler, Zittrain and Lessig are far from eloquent. Internet-
mediated freedom is a freedom to communication via the surrogate roots of
technological information and the reality they mediate.

In what follows I seek to analyse some of these issues by placing their
understanding within the context of fictional narrative. More specifically,
I attempt to explore, discuss and exemplify issues of action and symbolic
mediation by using a small fragment of *Invisible Cities*, a novel written by
Italo Calvino[3] that seems to me to capture the phenomena that concern
us here with unique force and evocation. Such a venture may seem long-
stretched yet the philosophical vision and penetrating insight into the
human condition of writers such as Calvino and Borges (Sarlo, 1993) more
than justifies the project of bringing fiction to bear on the understanding of
the puzzling issues raised by the deployment of human artifice in the project
of understanding and mediating the world. Fiction has, in addition, the
great merit of providing in one stroke a penetrating *in-sight* to the human
condition that may otherwise necessitate lengthy analytical exposure.

The present chapter is an attempt to open a vista of meaningful questions, not to reach any definitive conclusions. It both concludes the volume
and at the same time ushers, as any genuine conclusion should do, in new
issues that are associated with the multivalent involvement of information technology in human affairs. Overall, the part of Calvino's novel that
I present and comment on here is seen as an allegory of the vicissitudes and
paradoxes that are associated with the distancing from immediate contexts
and the human attempt to reconstruct, account for and control the world
through the vicarious character of standardized systems of signification of
which software-based information tokens are the currency of the age.

---

[3] Italo Calvino (1923–85) is one of the great novelists of the 20th century.

The imperial chess game

Invisible Cities is a complex, non-linear narrative that unfolds at two levels. One level involves the serial description of fictional cities (55 in number) that grouped in 11 thematic units (such as *cities and memory*, *city and signs*) follow one after the other. Each thematic group is introduced and followed by the encounters, in italicized writing, of the two major figures of the novel, the Chinese emperor Kublai Khan and the Venetian merchant Marco Polo.[4] In the imaginary and elliptic context of that novel, Marco Polo is or becomes an agent of Kublai Khan. Wandering across vast expanses of territory, Marco Polo returns periodically to the palace reporting to the emperor on the state of his empire. His reports of the empire, however, are not verbal descriptions, for they initially lack a common verbal medium. In the absence of a common language, the will to communicate cannot but pass through the signifying capacity of things and gestures:

> From the foot of the Great Kahn's throne a majolica pavement extended. Marco Polo, mute informant, spread out on it the samples of the wares he had brought back from his journeys to the ends of the empire: a helmet, a seashell, a coconut, a fan. Arranging the objects in a certain order on the black and white tiles, and occasionally shifting them with studied moves, the ambassador tried to depict for the monarch's eyes the vicissitudes of his travels, the conditions of the empire, the prerogatives of the distant provincial seats.

The lack of common language and the recourse to objects as the only means of communication is surely amenable to many interpretations. However, it gradually becomes evident as the novel unfolds that signification by objects is intended as a metaphor for apprehending those modes of acting and signifying which are still tied to immediacy. Calvino construes an imaginary, evolutionary trajectory whereby communication initially bears the heavy traces of contextual involvement. For all its clumsiness or limitations, object mediated signification is powerful and suggestive. It is the very physicality of things (e.g., a coconut, a seashell) and the particular function they embody (e.g., helmet, arrow) which becomes the carrier of semantic content. Signification by objects is inexorably tied to immediacy, the contexts in which objects have been encountered. For, though detached and removed from these contexts (after all, the things Marco Polo carries

---

[4] It is two of these encounters that I present and analyse in this chapter.

are just samples of wares), the meaning and the world that objects *qua* signs are supposed to communicate cannot emerge unless the *object itself possesses the characteristics which it purports to convey* (Goodman, 1976). A coconut may exemplify agriculture and the helmet an army but not the other way around. It is this intrinsic relationship to the contexts in which they have been encountered that empowers objects *qua* signs to convey or relate to aspects of these contexts.

I return to this issue many times over in what follows but let me meanwhile draw attention to what seems to me another crucial point in the passage, that is, Marco Polo's attempt to reconstruct his experience and convey his knowledge by arranging the objects in a *certain pattern*. It is not simply individual objects that signify but also their shifting combinations. This elementary *ars combinatoria* of the objects *qua* signs considerably expands what can be signified by each one of them separately. The emperor does not fail to observe this:

> Kublai Khan was a keen chess-player; following Marco's movements, he observed that certain pieces implied or excluded the vicinity of other pieces and were shifted along certain lines. Ignoring the object's variety of form, he could grasp the system of arranging one with respect to others on the majolica floor. He thought 'if each city is like a game of chess, the day when I have learned the rules, I shall finally possess my empire, even if I shall never succeed in knowing all the cities it contains'.

In a web of metaphors (i.e., the game of chess, signifying systems, and rules and connections), this passage reveals the increasing complexity of human signification as it proceeds from individual items to the construction of greater signifying blocks and systems. Sense, namely the construction of meaning, has traditionally been connected with the transition from reference to structure, from the external world to which a text or a composite semiotic construction makes references towards its interior.[5] As shown in the preceding chapter, there is a tension between sense and reference. Words or individual items in general combine into sentences and greater semiotic blocks whose meaningful content is driven away from the meaning and reference of individual items. The individuality of single items is reframed and at times overshadowed as their signifying content fuses and gradually dissolves into the totality of meaning constructed and conveyed by greater

---

[5] See the preceding chapter and also Barthes (1967, 1977), Leach (1976) and Ricoeur (1977, 1984).

signifying blocks. Beyond the signification of individual items, it is the very logic, the structure or the system through which individual elements bear upon one another which opens up the space of meaning and reveals how a particular system and the artefacts it helps to produce signify. Kublai Khan, a connoisseur of the workings of such systems (a keen chess player), did not fail to observe that 'certain pieces implied or excluded the vicinity of other pieces and were shifted along certain lines'.

Kublai Khan accordingly shifts his attention from individual objects and their separate significations towards the greater system formed by their combinations. But it is not particular combinations either which are the main interest of his concern, but the generative rules, that is, the *ars combinatoria*, which lead to the object-made relationships and combinations manifested on each occasion. Individual objects and their instantiated combinations are no more than cues or means for grasping the rules which lead to the essential knowledge of the empire. The very image of the empire that results from the knowledge and application of the generative rules gains precedence over what such an image is supposed to refer to. Knowledge of the rules represents, it would seem, a special kind of knowledge, for it is concerned with mastery and control rather than disinterested reconstruction for the sake of knowing: 'the day when I have learned the rules, I shall finally possess my empire, even if I shall never succeed in knowing all the cities it contains.' Taken together the passages above seem to imply the following:

- Objects are signs or symbols used as elements in a signifying system that conveys the experiences of the merchant.
- Objects signify thanks to the intrinsic relationship they have to the contexts to which they refer.
- Objects *qua* signs can be related to one another and combined into chains that exemplify, communicate and represent diverse states of the empire.
- Combinations of objects follow a *system* which, though relying on the signifying appearance and individuality of these objects, goes beyond them.
- The system is generated and dissolved according to certain rules; it is these *generative rules*, neither the objects nor even the system, that constitute the essential knowledge of the empire.

The picture of signification and communication that emerges from the first two passages is one whereby discrete, individual *elements* can be *combined* into greater units according to certain *rules*. It is a view that in essential points re-echoes the fundamentals of signification and communication, including technical models of meaning generation and transmission. Meaning can be traced back to a certain number of single or elementary units (symbol tokens) which can be related and combined following certain rules (algorithms) to form larger signifying structures.[6] However, two fundamental tensions lurk behind that view of communication Calvino conveys in these two passages. The first is the tension between individual elements versus the combinations to which they can enter. The second is the contrast between the instantiation produced by any combination of elements versus the generativity of the rules through which the elements are combined and the inexhaustive capacity of the rules to produce new combinations.[7] The picture therefore gradually becomes subtler, more complex and elusive, and it is therefore important to follow its slippery path. Relying on his observation of Polo's arrangements, Kublai Khan ponders over whether to replace the merchant's idiosyncratic system of representation with the ready-made and standardized world of the game of chess.

> Actually, it was useless for Marco's speeches to employ all this bric-a-brac: a chessboard would have sufficed, with its specific pieces. To each piece, in turn, they could give an appropriate meaning: a knight could stand for a real horseman, or for a procession of coaches, an army on the march, an equestrian monument; a queen could be a lady looking down from her balcony, a fountain, a church with a pointed dome, a quince tree.

Kublai Khan's comparison of Marco Polo's object-mediated and idiosyncratic discourse with the quadrangular and standardized world of the chessboard and the chessmen can be read, I suggest, as a figurative way of describing the tension between context-embedded and abstract signification, between, on the one hand, the concrete and particular and, on the other hand, the general and universal. In the eyes of the leader, far removed from the action contexts of the empire, Marco Polo's discourse appears as useless bric-a-brac, too much mired in detail and specificity and all the constraints these last carry. It is on the contrary the standardized world of the game of chess and the designations of chessmen yet to be agreed upon that could provide the possibility of reconstructing the facts and states of the empire.

---

[6] See Kallinikos (1998) and Ekbia (2008) for a critical summary of some of the ideas that have haunted *Artificial Intelligence*. To some degree one can discern in Calvino's initial portrait of communication key tenets of *structuralism*, which during the period Calvino wrote his novel was at the crossroads of many intellectual debates.
[7] Generativity is an essential quality of human language (see, e.g., Searle, 2010).

However, the potential designations of the signifying elements (the chessmen) remain ambiguous in a fashion that differs from the silent ambiguity of Marco Polo's objects. For, whereas the latter could be thought as indicators, samples of the contexts in which they had been encountered, the chessmen's potential signifying ability extends over and embraces a multitude of phenomena: for example, a 'queen' could signify everything from a lady looking down from her balcony to a quince tree. And whereas the connection of 'queen' and 'lady' might be looked upon as alluding to an intrinsic (feminine) relationship between sign and referent, the affinities become more vague and distant in the other designations. In contrast to signification by thing-objects, standardized embodiments of meaning break with similarity as a signifying principle. Intrinsic relationships between the sign and the referent are too much tied to immediate contexts and must therefore be redeemed from the heavy traces of reality they carry to assume their standardized signifying function.

The transition to the standardized character of the game of chess suggests that the replacement of experiential knowledge (here Marco Polo's ways of signifying through objects) and the means by which it is conveyed by a formalized and decontextualized system of signification does not necessarily follow the logic of empirical incrementalism. Even though the homologies between Marco Polo's object-made discourse and the game of chess are obvious, the latter involves a transition to a standardized system already in use. Actually, it is by means of the game of chess that Kublai Khan perceives and understands the peculiar combinations of the objects, rather than the other way around. Experiential knowledge is not simply transcribed or translated into another system but replaced and disregarded. Overall, the transition to the game of chess implies that the initial objects that bear the traces of the merchant's adventures, and have literally been involved in the contexts and sequences they attempt to reconstruct, are abandoned and replaced by the standardized appearance of chessmen, and their combinations dictated by an equally well delineated and standardized repertoire of rules.

The game of chess could thus be interpreted as a series of metaphors that seek to exemplify the puzzling questions and paradoxes involved in the ascent from the concrete and individual to the abstract, from context-embedded actions and meanings to standardized and decontextualized representations. Standardization always implies a disregard for the singular and contingent and a corresponding concern for the common and recurrent. Though the evolutionary path from immediacy to abstraction might be said to involve the entire history of mankind (Cassirer, 1955), awareness of the questions involved sheds new light on the cognitive and communication issues that I associate with technological mediation and the Internet. Modern societies witness innumerable times the social and episte-mological steps and consequences of such a radical transition, on each occa-sion that a novel empirical domain is singled out and lifted from the edges of social life and the informal relations it is embedded to become visible and institutionalized, the object of representation (Hacking, 1983).

Following the trajectory of the whole narrative and drawing on what has been said so far, I would like to suggest that the passages referred to so far provide a nexus of metaphors that recaptures part of the issues and ques-tions related to *the transition from an immediate system of signification still tied to sensations and objects qua signs to an abstract and disembodied language.* Selective objectification distances itself from worldly references and creates skew relationships with aspects of reality which attempts either to account for or create. Representation breaks with similarity as a basic form of des-ignation. Or to put it otherwise, designation by similarity or any other kind of intrinsic relationship is over-constraining, by being always tied to immediacy and the exterior world. The controlling and surveying attitude of representation needs to and does dispense with these constraints. The intrinsic relationships of similarity or affinity are traded off for a worked-out and stipulated system of designations and combinatorial rules. But the chal-lenge persists. Such a representing system must first demonstrate its ability to capture and reconstitute the diversity of the empire:

> Returning from his last mission, Marco Polo found the Khan awaiting him, seated at a chessboard. With a gesture he invited the Venetian to sit opposite him and describe, with the help only of the chessmen, the cities he had visited. Marco did not lose heart. The Great Khan's chessmen were huge pieces of polished ivory: arranging on the board looming rooks and sulky knights, assembling swarms of pawns, drawing straight or oblique avenues like a queen's progress, Marco re-created the perspectives and the spaces of black and white cities on moonlit nights.

The way to standardized representation captured by the metaphor of the game of chess as a signifying medium is prepared and decided by the leader, for it would seem to fit better his detached position and his controlling preoccupations. The agent, on the other hand, seems to have no choice but to rely on it (the game of chess) to recount his knowledge and experience of the empire. The task is not easy but 'Marco did not lose heart.' Employing the standardized significations of the chessmen and relying on the rules of the game he 're-created' the subtle states of the empire. 'The Great Khan's chessmen were huge pieces of polished ivory' which seems again to suggest a complex maze of metaphors and allusions. For, in contrast to objects or natural signs, the pieces of polished ivory are elaborate human constructions. Both 'polished' and 'ivory' hint at the precious – and reflecting? – character of these elements and, perhaps, at the fact that they are the cumulative product of long and enduring human effort. As 'huge' they are imposing and probably not easily manipulable. Standardized systems of signification and the institutions into which they are embedded constrain expression with the same means by which they enable it (Bateson, 1972; Douglas, 1986). Standardization is both a valuable resource and a powerful constraint. Bereft of his object-signs, Marco Polo's knowledge has no other way of reaching beyond himself, except through the deployment of the common and standardized world of the game of chess the emperor offers him.

For Kublai Khan, the leader, the situation is different. It is precisely the road away from the contingent and particular towards the enduring and systemic that gives his detached position the ability to control his empire. As Calvino's penetrating prose makes clear, control and knowledge do not necessarily coincide. Put differently, they constitute different breeds of human knowing geared to different projects and purposes. For that reason, the mediation of details and local situations that detract from the task of compiling the bigger picture must give way to regularities that cut across particular contexts, helping the emperor to control his empire. In the different perspectives, interests and experiences of the novel's main figures one could perhaps recognize the fundamental tension between, on the one hand, the requirements of decontextualized knowledge and representation and, on the other, the characteristics of context-embedded modes of involvement and signification. Communication and involvement that rely on the principles of similarity and proximity are too immersed in details to be able to capture the wider picture and they have accordingly to give way to the superior signifying ability of distancing representation (Goodman, 1976, 1978). However, such a transition is not an unambiguous leap forward. Trading off detail and contingency for standardization does not come without a cost. Various complications begin already to emerge:

> Contemplating these essential landscapes, Kublai reflected on the invisible order that sustains cities, on the rules that decreed how they rise, take shape and prosper, adapting themselves to the seasons, and then how they sadden and fall in ruins. At times he thought he was on the verge of discovering a coherent, harmonious system underlying the infinite deformities and discords, but no model could stand up to the comparison

with the game of chess. Perhaps, instead of racking one's brain to suggest with the ivory pieces' scant help visions which were anyway destined to oblivion, it would suffice to play a game according to the rules and to consider each successive state of the board as one of the countless forms that the system of forms assembles and destroys.

I have earlier drawn attention to the difference between systemic relationships and the specific application of rules whereby such relationships are produced. The generativity of rules, the *ars combinatoria* of the representational elements and the vast number of signifying options that can thus be generated, are explicitly contrasted with the notion of system and the model whereby it can be conveyed: 'no model could stand up to the comparison with the game of chess.' For, whereas a system or a model could be looked upon as a fixed and frozen arrangement of elements, the effectuation of a possibility, rules provide a wide space of possibilities whose realization seems to unfold along distinct but not determinate paths. Rules are, so to speak, constitutive but not determinative of the game (Searle, 1995) and in being so they are generative.[8] They are not exhausted by their particular applications. As a metaphor for representation, the standardized and closed-upon-itself world of the game of chess reveals the resilient character and the almost unlimited capacity of representational systems to produce a vast number of versions that capture or can be used to refer to the incessantly shifting state of the world.

Game rules, however, concern relationships between the representational elements themselves, not the particular designations, the worldly references of individual elements. They are combinatorial principles that prescribe the conditions under which certain elements can be combined with others and are thus far removed from the tangible world. Rules have meaning but are obviously devoid of denotative content. They do not stand for something 'out there'. Rules are about the game, they concern the game itself. The application of rules, then, implies that individual elements signify – mean and refer – by entering into networks of fabricated, that is, conceived and established, relationships. Objectified and institutionalized principles of combination (rules) are by this oblique route involved in the construction of the world. Fascinated by the possibilities opened by the game of chess,

---

[8] It is perhaps worth relating Calvino's portrayal of the game of the chess and the metaphors he spins out around it with Zittrain's (2008) description of the generative nature of the Internet I mentioned in the introduction of this chapter. See also Kallinikos, Aaltonen & Marton, (2010).

Kublai Khan takes a further step into the disembodied yet promising, as he thinks, world of standardized representation:

> Now Kublai Khan no longer had to send Marco Polo on distant expeditions: he kept him playing endless games of chess. Knowledge of the empire was hidden in the pattern drawn by the angular shifts of the knight, by the diagonal passages opened by the bishop's incursions, by the lumbering, cautious tread of the king and the humble pawn, by the inexorable ups and downs of every game.

The transition from Marco Polo's object-mediated discourse to the standardized world of the game of chess, from context-embedded knowledge to decontextualized representation is thus consummated. Marco Polo does not have to visit the empire any longer. For, ironically perhaps, the knowledge of the empire is implicated in the finite number of representational elements and the set of rules that govern their combinations. The metaphor recaptures the epistemological steps which the transition from the concrete to the abstract and the irreversible turning away from immediacy and context-embeddedness imply. It also recounts, in the suggestive language of fiction, essential aspects of the previous chapter as well as the debate surrounding the developmental trajectory of information and communication technologies from its early stages to the Internet.[9]

The knowledge once gained by the agent's expeditions, his direct confrontation with facts and situations is no longer relevant for the emperor. Either has it to be transcribed and codified into a finite number of disjoint elements whose combinations are governed by a pre-given repertoire of rules or completely abandoned. The fact that knowledge of the empire is implicated in the combinatorial rules of the representational elements suggests again an intrinsic tension between sense and reference that I explored in some detail in the preceding chapter. For, whereas sense is definitively dependent on the direct application of rules and is therefore drawn towards the interior, as it were, of representation, reference obeys a centrifugal movement and demands reality anchorage.

The limits of representation

The radical step implied by Kublai Khan's decision to make a chess player out of an explorer can be interpreted to suggest that standardized

[9]See, for example, Borgmann (1999), Brook and Boal (1995), Dreyfus (2001), Dreyfus and Dreyfus (1986), Flachbart and Weibel (2005), Hayles (2005, 2006), Terzidis (2006), Zuboff (1988).

representation cannot exist except by turning its back to the concrete and tangible world. Such a remarkable shift is, however, not free of problems and perplexities. The gains are not acquired for nothing:

> The Great Khan tried to concentrate on the game: but now it was the game's reason that eluded him. The end of every game is a gain or a loss: but of what? What were the real stakes? At checkmate beneath the foot of the king, knocked aside by the winner's hand, nothingness remains: a black square, or a white one. By disembodying his conquests to reduce them to the essential, Kublai had arrived at the extreme operation: the definitive conquest, of which the empire's multiform treasures were illusory envelopes; it was reduced to a square of planed wood.

The urge for an essential world drives the transition from the concrete to the abstract and implies, the leap into a void and disembodied world. The *other* of the bulky, concrete and refractory state of things is an elusive and empty being. Calvino captures here the paradoxical relationship between sense and reference. The game's reason eluded the emperor. Sense and meaning cannot totally dispense with reference. Even if sense is a question to be answered by the interior texture of a symbol system, a fuller appreciation of what is posited in representation creates a centrifugal movement towards reference to reality. Such a problem would, of course, have never appeared had the representational elements maintained unambiguous and demarcated references to reality. But the road, as we have seen, from things to words, from the molten and messy reality to representation and vice versa is a long and crooked one. Neither individual elements nor representation as a system (or discourse) recaptures and refers to tangible totalities. Had that being the case, the disembodied world of representation would have then had a definitive anchoring into the solidity of things, and meaning would have been clear and transparent but also bound and to some degree truncated. Representation gains its signifying valence by dispensing with similarity and intrinsic relations as signifying conventions. As suggested earlier, the powerful signifying capacity of standardized elements result from them having being redeemed from any vestiges of reality and attuned to the other signifying elements in ways that enable the application of rules through which they are assembled to greater signifying units. Such a step proves now ambiguous. The distancing from the plenitude of reality runs the risk of hollowing out purpose and meaning from the inside.

The liberation thus of representation from the bounds of refractory reality, and signification by means of a tidy and standardized system seem to be bought at the price of emptiness. The *nothingness* confronting Kublai Khan 'beneath the foot of the king, knocked aside by the winner's hand,' is the result of successive abstractions conveyed by elements whose materiality cannot and does not coincide with that of the referent. The question of reference cannot be exhausted and fully grasped by falling back onto individual elements. For these last are not any longer tied to reality as object *qua* signs do. They are just elements of a complex signifying machine. Rather than having simple and unambiguous one-to-one correspondences to reality, representational elements gain their signifying space through a complex and ramifying network of relationships with other representational elements.

As it turns out, Kublai Khan becomes the cognitive victim of his own quest to control and the disembodied signification that he has helped establish. The same leader that conceived and initiated the transition to an abstract and decontextualized system stands bewildered in front of the relationship of representation to the things it refers, and cannot rediscover the connection between the representing elements and the reality to which they are supposed to refer. The effacement of the tangible world, consequent upon its reduction to a standardized system of signification and its foundations (just 'a square of planed wood') impinges upon sense and meaning and calls for re-establishing the connections between symbol tokens and reality, sign and referent. It is Marco Polo's experiential knowledge that provides the means for re-establishing such a connection and breathing life back into the disembodied world of representation:

> Then Marco Polo spoke: 'Your chessboard, sir, is inlaid with two woods: ebony and maple. The square on which your enlightened gaze is fixed was cut from the ring of a trunk that grew in a year of drought: you see how its fibres are arranged? Here a barely hinted knot can be made out: a bud tried to burgeon on a premature spring day, but the night's frost forced it to desist.'
>
> Until then the Great Khan had not realized that the foreigner knew how to express himself fluently in his languages, but it was not this fluency that amazed him.
>
> 'Here is a thicker pore: perhaps it was a larvum's nest; not a woodworm, because, once born, it would have begun to dig, but a caterpillar that gnawed the leaves and was the cause of the tree's being chosen for chopping down ... This edge was scored by the wood-carver with his gouge so that it would adhere to the next square, more protruding ...'

Such is the plenitude of 'refractory' reality for those that can read it. A small number of signs, imprinted upon the material constitution of the wood, can provide the starting point for a semantic journey that allows an entire (absent) world to reappear. Here, sense and reference seem to reinforce one another. For, upon the apparent simplicity of the wood, the nothingness which puzzles and bewilders Kublai Khan, are left the traces of a multitude of events, ranging from natural conditions to human practices. All those minutia of life that standardized representation overlooks, obscures or relegates to trivia can be summoned to support purpose and meaning. Lost no wonder in the compactness of wood texture, these details can be brought to the fore and deciphered only by the sharp and experienced eye. The road back to reality passes, then, through the labyrinthine structure of signs engraved upon the very materiality of the elements and conventions that constitute standardized representation.

In the metaphor of the game of chess, the apparent nothingness of the black and white tiles of the chessboard nonetheless supports the chessmen, that is, the signifying elements, and allows for the realization of rules through which these elements are combined. The disembodied gaze of representation is haunted by past actions and foregone events, disregarded details, overlooked facts and contingencies that Derrida once construed as the alterity and absence essential to meaning that *prima facie* presents itself as clear and self-sufficient (Derrida, 1978, 1982). All this foregone reality can be vicariously restituted but not grasped. In Calvino's imaginative literary accomplishment, the limits of representation appear as the limits not of a copy view of knowledge but of a worldview that conceives, posits and acts upon the world by means of its distancing and fabricated categories, and the elements that convey them. Representation and abstraction seem ready to dissolve into the succession of events by means of which they have been constituted and the reassertion of those details once crossed out as irrelevant by the tidy logic of standardization. Sense and reference here reinforce one another as the traces of an expelled reality are summoned to breathe life back to the imminent hollowness of standardized representation.

It is Marco Polo and not Kublai Kahn who knows how to find the crooked path that leads back from the abstract to the concrete, from standardization to reality and from representation to reference. Deciphering the signs, Polo is able to retrace the sequence of events lying silent and hidden behind the simplicity and muteness of the wood. In contrast to the detached leader, his remarkable ability to discern the texture of events that resulted in the making of the chessboard is connected with his substantial knowledge of human dealings, gained through confrontation with facts and situations and long experiential involvement (his travels to the empire). For, the details he is able to summon are the details which only engagement, experience and practice can support. It seems paradoxical, yet abstract forms of knowing both negate and rely on situated knowledge. A fuller interpretation of abstract statements or systems seems possible only in the background of local, experiential knowledge.[10]

All this can be done, however, thanks to the signifying medium of verbal language by which the Venetian merchant is able to disclose to the emperor the rich and semantically dense world of real life. Language is here given the central role it has in human life and practice, a potent medium and system able to embrace and translate any other system of signification into its own terms, a carrier but also constitutive force of reality (Barthes, 1967; Eco, 1976; Searle, 2010). For, while an adversary to reality, in the sense of ultimately been a system of signs and rules, language is at the same time the offspring of the human confrontation with reality and the miraculous artifice by means of which reality is sensed, known, expanded and acted upon. Neither logic nor measurement is possible without the semantics of language.[11] It is out of that semantics that all other human techniques and conventions of signifying and representing are born and towards which they converge. Not surprisingly, the road back to the world is and cannot but be but a *verbal* one:

> The quantity of things that could be read in a little piece of smooth and empty wood overwhelmed Kublai; Polo was already talking about ebony forests, about rafts laden with logs that come down the rivers, of docks, of women at the windows ...

Final remarks

In this chapter I have used Italo Calvino's imaginative prose from *Invisible Cities* and the metaphor of the game of chess as shortcut to some of the issues raised by standardized representation. Standardization in meaning production and communication emerges out of the inescapable disregard of the particular and through subsuming the diversity and variability of reality to recurring types and categories. In this process, an inevitable friction is generated between the signifying potency of standardized representation and its frail connection to the reality to which it seeks to refer, construct or control.

This friction, I suggest, takes its most typical contemporary form in the case of software and the data tokens produced and circulated by the standards, rules and procedures characteristic of software technology. It acquires more profound dimensions by the expansion of the Internet and the understanding of reality it compels through detached information tokens.

---

[10] See Esposito (2004).

[11] Captured by the Greek *logos* in which the meanings of *speech* and *reason* harmoniously coexist.

The Internet is, of course, anything else than a tidy and standardized system of representation. Extended regions of the deep Internet are undeniably composed of software-based techniques for organizing and ordering data and information. Much of what we are able to experience through the Internet would have been impossible without the far-reaching standardization through which data and information tokens are organized, processed and transmitted. And yet, at some other level, the Internet is a transient, incessantly shifting, digital disorder (Weinberger, 2007) of unprecedented dimensions, a jumble of nearly everything that Michael Benedikt (1991) prophetically described, two decades ago at its very onset, as a world of data and lies, knowledge and memories of nature. But as in the world of the game of chess, the promises and deceptions of which Calvino's prose nicely captures, the jumble of the Internet is made possible through the radical disconnection from reality. It is that disconnection which the plenitude of reality repeatedly challenges, providing at the same time a strong reminiscence of the limits of that venture and the tidiness, standardization and ultimately illusion underlying it (Flusser, 2000, 2002).[12]

It is against the background of these considerations that I view Italo Calvino's imaginative prose and the small extract from *Invisible Cities* I have presented and commented in this chapter an evocative illustration of some critical issues raised by the Internet and the comprehensive data grid that results from the growing confluence and synergy of information systems and artefacts. The signifying output of standardized representation is, obviously, recontextualized and reinterpreted as it becomes immersed in human affairs and the pursuits of social agents. Many readers may raise their eyebrows at what they may see as a sweeping generalization of what the Internet is and does. And yet, the possibilities of re-appropriating and recontextualizing information are heavily conditioned by the signifying output, the rules and conventions that govern standardized representation. In the case of the contemporary technologies of computing and communication and the Internet, the opportunity of re-appropriation of contextual reality is furthermore diminished, rather radically, by the fact that the cognitive output that is presented at the human interface is the outcome of long driven automation from which humans are, in one way or another, excluded.

In this respect, the narrative section of the *Invisible Cities* presented here is intended as a parable of the Internet and the many and ambiguous ties it maintains with reality as well as the mixed blessings it brings. The Internet

---

[12] See Nardi and Kow (2010) for a recent and evocative account of the Internet and the illusory reality it conveys.

has so far predominantly been understood and analysed as platform of communication and action. Though occasionally observed the implications its diffusion has for the less obvious issues of how we understand and relate to reality have by and large remained in the margins of the limelight, commented, alluded to but, with few exceptions (e.g., Borgmann, 1999, 2010; Dreyfus, 2001), seldom analysed in a systematic fashion. To a certain degree this is understandable; even more so if the trend towards standardized modes of signification and communication is seen as the inescapable and irrevocable accompaniment of modes of living as ours that daily span the earthly universe, the ups and downs of nations and markets, the occurrence of natural disasters, wars, sports games, Hollywood parties and celebrities gossiping, iPad launches, and the likes. How much of this expanded reality can one really know by acquaintance and experience? Perhaps we are the last generation to raise issues of this sort. And yet something is irredeemably lost behind 'the glamorous fog of cyberspace', as Albert Borgmann poignantly (2010) refers to it. In this chapter as well as in the entire volume I have attempted to offer a sober exposition as to why this is or may be the case, and disclose the forms through which the huge artifice of technology enables and constrains our lives, gives us with one hand what its other hand reclaims.

References

Adorno, T. W. (1973). *Negative Dialectics*. London: Routledge. Originally published in Germany in 1966.

Adorno, T. W. (1984). *Aesthetic Theory*. London: Routledge.

Allen, J. P. (2005). 'Value Conflicts in Enterprise Systems', *Information Technology and People*, 18/1: 33–49.

Anderson, C. (2008). 'The End of Theory', *Wired*, July 2008.

Anderson J. R. (1983). *The Architecture of Cognition*. Cambridge, Ma: Harvard University Press.

Arnold, M. (2003). 'On the Phenomenology of Technology: The "Janus-faces" of Mobile Phones', *Information and Organization*, 13, 231–56.

Arthur, B. W. (1994). *Increasing Returns and Path Dependence in the Economy*. Ann Arbor: The University of Michigan Press.

Arthur, B. W. (2009). *The Nature of Technology*. London: Alen Lane (Penguin).

Avgerou, C. (2002). *Information Systems and Global Diversity*. Oxford: Oxford University Press.

Avital, M. and Vandenbosch, B. (2000). 'SAP Implementation at Metalica; An Organizational Drama in Two Acts', *Journal of Information Technology*, 15/3: 183–94.

Bagozzi, R. B. (2007). 'The Legacy of the Technology Acceptance Model and a Proposal for a Paradigm Shift', *Journal of the Association of Information Systems*, 8/4: 244–54.

Bancroft, N. H., Seip, H. & Sprengel, A. (1996) *Implementing SAP R/3*. Greenwich: Manning.

Barthes, R. (1967). *Elements of Sociology*. New York: Noonday.

Barthes, R. (1977). *Image, Music, Text*. New York: Hill and Windg.

Bateson, G. (1972). *Steps to an Ecology of Mind*. New York: Ballantine.

Beck, U. (1992). *Risk Society: Towards a New Modernity*. London: Sage.

Benedikt, M. (ed.) (1991). *Cyberspace: First Steps*. Cambridge, Mass.: MIT Press.

Beniger, J. (1986). *The Control Revolution: Technological and Economic Origins of the Information Society*. Cambridge, Mass.: Harvard University Press.

Benkler, Y. (2006). *The Wealth of Networks: How Social Production Transforms Market and Freedom*. New Haven: Yale University Press and http://www.benkler.org. Accessed on 23 August 2010.

Bijker, B. (2001) 'Understanding Technological Culture through a Constructivist View of Science, Technology and Culture', in S. Cutcliffe & C. Mitcham (eds), *Visions of STS: Counterpoints in Science, Technology and Society Studies*. New York: State University of New York.

Bijker, W. E, Hughes, T. P. & Pinch, T. (eds) (1987). *The Social Construction of Technological Systems*. Cambridge, Ma: The MIT Press.

Bloomfield, B. & Vurdubakis, T. (2001). 'The Vision Thing: Construction of Time and Technology in Management Advice', in T. Clark & R. Fincham (eds), *Critical Consulting: Perspectives on the Management Advice Industry*. Oxford: Blackwell.

Boland, R. J. (1987). 'The In-formation of Information Systems', in R. J. Boland and R. Hirschheim (eds), *Critical Issues in Information Systems Research*, New York: Wiley.

Bolter, J. D. (1991). *The Writing Space: The Computer, Hypertext and the History of Writing*. Hillsdale: LEA.

Bolter, D. J. and Gruzin, R. (2002). *Remediation: Understanding New Media*. Cambridge, Mass.: MIT Press.

Borgmann, A. (1984). *Technology and the Character of Contemporary Life*. Chicago: The University of Chicago Press

Borgmann, A. (1992). *Crossing the Postmodern Divide*. Chicago: The University of Chicago Press.

Borgmann, A. (1999). *Holding on to Reality: The Nature of Information at the Turn of the Millennium*. Chicago: The University of Chicago Press.

Borgmann, A. (2010). 'Orientation in Technological Space', *First Monday*, 15: 6–7, June.

Bowker, G. and Star, S. L (1999). *Sorting Things Out: Classification and its Consequences*. Cambridge, Mass: The MIT Press.

Brook, J. and Boal, I. (1995). *Resisting the Virtual Life*. San Francisco: City Lights.

Brooks, F. P. (1987). 'No Silver Bullet: Essence and Accidents of Software Engineering', *Computer*, 20/4: 10–19.

Burchell, G., Gordon, C. and Miller, P. (eds) (1991). *The Foucault Effect: Studies in Governmentality*. Chicago: The University of Chicago Press.

Burke, K. (1966). *Language as Symbolic Action*. Berkeley: University of California Press.

Burke, K. (1981). 'The Interactive Bind', in C. Wilder-Mott & J. Weekland (eds), *Rigor and Imagination: Essays on the Legacy of Gregory Bateson*. New York: Preyer.

Cadili, S. and Whitley, E. W. (2005). 'On the Interpretive Flexibility of Hosted ERP Systems', *Journal of Strategic Information Systems*, 14/2: 167–95.

Calvino, I. (1974). *Invisible Cities*. San Diego: Harcourt Brace Jovanovich.

Cassirer, E. (1955). *The Philosophy of Symbolic Forms: Vol. 1: language*. New Haven: Yale University Press.

Castells, M. (1996). *The Rise of Network Society*. Oxford: Blackwell.

Castells, M. (2000). 'Materials for an Explanatory Theory of the Network Society', *British Journal of Sociology*, 51(1): 5–24.

Castells, M. (2001). *The Internet Galaxy*. Oxford: Oxford University Press.

Castoriadis, C. (1987). *The Imaginary Institution of Society*. Stanford: Stanford University Press.

Chandler, A. D. (1962). *Strategy and Structure*. Cambridge, Mass: The MIT Press.

Chandler, A. D. (1977). *The Visible Hand*. Cambridge, Mass: The MIT Press.

Ciborra, C. U. (1993). *Teams, Markets and Systems*. Cambridge: Cambridge University Press.

Ciborra, C. U. (1996). 'The Platform Organization: Recombining Strategies, Structures, and Surprises', *Organization Science*, 7/2: 103–18.

Ciborra, C. U. (ed.) (1996). *Groupware and Teamwork*. New York: Wiley.

Ciborra, C. U. (1999) 'Notes on Time and Improvisation', *Accounting, Management and Information Technologies*, 9/1: 77–94.

Ciborra, C. U. (ed.) (2000). *From Control to Drift: The Dynamics of Corporate Information Infrastructures*. Oxford: Oxford University Press.

Ciborra, C. U. and Hanseth, O. (1988). 'From Tools to Gestell. Agendas for Managing Information Infrastructures', *Information, Technology and People*, 11/4: 305–27.

Ciborra, C. U. and Lanzara, G. F. (1994). 'Formative Contexts and Information Technology', *Accounting, Management and Information Technologies*, 4: 611–26.

Cline-Cohen, P. (1982). *A Calculating People: The Spread of Numeracy in Early America*. Chicago: The University of Chicago Press.

Contini, F. and Lanzara, G. F. (2009). *ICT and Innovation in the Public Sector: European Studies in the Making of E-Government*. New York: Palgrave Macmillan.

Cooper, R. (1989). 'The Visibility of Social Systems', in M. C. Jackson, P. Keys & S. A. Cropper (eds), *Operational Research and the Social Sciences*, New York: Plenum, pp. 51–7.

Cooper, R. and Kallinikos, J. (eds) (1996). 'Writing, Rationality and Organization', *Scandinavian Journal of Management*, Special issue, 12/1: 1–108.

Crozier, M. (2007). 'Recursive Governance: Contemporary Political Communication and Public Policy', *Political Communication*, 24/1: 1–18.

Crozier, M. (2010). 'Rethinking Systems: Configurations of Politics and Policy in Contemporary Governance', *Administration and Society*, 16 July 2010 DOI: 10.1177/0095399710377443. Accessed on 23 August 2010.

Cutcliffe, S. and Mitcham, C. (eds) (2001). *Visions of STS: Counterpoints in Science, Technology and Society Studies*. New York: State University of New York.

Derrida, J. (1978). *Writing and Difference*. London: Routledge.

Derrida, J. (1982). 'Sending: On Representation', *Social Research*, 49: 295–326, Special Issue on French Philosophy.

DiMaggio, P. (ed) (2001). *The Twenty-First Century Firm: Changing Economic Organization in International Perspective*. Princeton University Press.

Doherty, N. F., Coombs, C. R. and Loan-Clarke, J. (2006). 'A Reconceptualization of the Interpretive Flexibility of Information Technologies: Redressing the Balance between the Social and the Technical', *European Journal of Information Systems*, 15/6: 569–82.

Douglas, M. (1986). *How Institutions Think*. Syracuse: Syracuse University Press.

Dreyfus, H. (2001). *On the Internet*. London: Routledge.

Dreyfus, H. and Dreyfus, S. (1986). *Mind Over Machine*. New York: Free Press.

Eco, U. (1976). *A Theory of Semiotics*. Bloomington: Indiana University Press.

Ekbia, H. (2008). *Artificial Dreams*. Cambridge: Cambridge University Press.

Ellul, J. (1964). *The Technological Society*. New York: Vintage Books.

Engestrom, Y. (2001). 'Expansive Learning at Work: Toward an Activity Theoretical Reconceptualization', *Journal of Education and Work*, 14/1: 133–56.

Engestrom, Y. and Middleton, D. (1996). *Cognition and Communication at Work*. Cambridge University Press, Cambridge.

Erikson, E. H. (1977) *Toys and Reasons*. London: Marion Boyars.

Esposito, E. (2004). 'The Arts of Contingency', *Critical Inquiry*, 31, http://criticalinquiry.uchicago.edu/features/artsstatements/arts.esposito.htm. Accessed on 23 August 2010.

Esposito, E. (2011). *The Future of Futures. The Time of Money in Society and Finance*. Cheltenham: Elgar, (forthcoming). See also *Il futuro dei futures. Il tempo del denaro nella finanza and nella società*, ETS, Pisa, 2009 (Original publication) and *Die Zukunft der futures. Die Zeit des Geldes im Finanzwesen und in der Gesellschaft*, Carl Auer Verlag, Heidelberg, 2010 (German Translation).

Fan, M., Stallaert, J. and Whinston, A. B. (2000). 'The Adoption and Design Methodologies of Component-Based Enterprise Systems', *European Journal of Information Systems* 9: 25-35.

Feldman, J. (1986). 'On the difficulty of Learning from Experience', in H. P. Sims & D. A. Gioia (eds), *The Thinking Organization*, San Francisco: Jossey-Bass, pp. 263–92.

Feldman, M. S. and Pentland, B. T. (2003). 'Reconceptualizing Routines as a Source of Flexibility and Change', *Administrative Science Quarterly*, 48/1: 94–118.

Fleck, J. (1994). 'Learning by Trying: The Implementation of Configurational Technology', *Research Policy*, 23: 637–52.

Flachbart, G. and Weibel, P. (2005) (eds). *Disappearing Architecture: From Real to Virtual to Quantum*. Boston: Birkhhauser.

Flusser, V. (2000). *Towards a Philosophy of Photography*. London: Reaktion Books.

Flusser, V. (2002). *Writings*. Minneapolis: University of Minnesota Press.

Foucault, M. (1970). *The Order of Things*. London: Tavistock.

Foucault, M. (1977). *Discipline and Punish: The Birth of the Prison*. London: Penguin.

Foucault, M. (1991). 'Politics and the Study of Discourse', in G. Burtchell, C. Gordon & P. Miller (eds), *The Foucault Effect*. Oxford: Harvester, pp. 52–72.

Francalanci, C. (2001). 'Predicting the Implementation Effort of ERP Projects: Empirical Evidence on SAP/R3', *Journal of Information Technology*, 16/1: 33–48.

Frege, G. (1950). *The Foundations of Arithmetic*. Oxford: Blackwell.

Freidson, E. (2001). *Professionalism: The Third Logic*. Cambridge: Polity.

Friedland, R. and Alford, R. R. (1991). 'Bringing Society Back In: Symbols, Practices, and Institutional Contradictions', in W. W. Powell and P. J. DiMaggio (eds), *The New Institutionalism in Organizational Analysis*, Chicago: University of Chicago Press, pp. 232–63.

Gellner, E. (1995). *Conditions of Liberty: Civil Society and its Rivals*. London: Penguin.

Goffman, E. (1974). *Frame Analysis*. Harper: New York.

Goodman, N. (1976). *Languages of Art*. Indianapolis: Hackett.

Goodman, N. (1978). *Ways of Worldmaking*. Indianapolis: Hackett.

Goody, J. (1986). *The Logic of Writing and the Organization of Society*. Cambridge: Cambridge University Press.

Grimmelmann, J. (2005). 'Regulation by Software', *The Yale Law Journal*, 114: 1719–58.

Grint, K. and Woolgar, S. (1992). 'Computers, Guns and Roses: What's Social about Being Shot?', *Science, Technology and Human Values*, 17/3: 366–80.

Grint, K. and Woolgar, S. (1997). *The Machine at Work: Technology, Work and Organization*. Cambridge: Polity Press.

Göranzon, B. (1992). *The Practical Intellect: Computers and Human Skills*. London: Springer Verlag.

Hacking, I. (1983). *Representing and Intervening*. Cambridge: Cambridge University Press.

Hacking, I. (1999). *The Social Construction of What?* Cambridge, Mass: The Harvard University Press.

Hanseth, O. (2000). 'The Economics of Standards', in C. Ciborra (ed.), *From Control to Drift: The Dynamics of Corporate Information Infrastructures*. Oxford: Oxford University Press.

Hanseth, O. (2004). 'Knowledge as Infrastructure', in C. Avgerou, C. Ciborra & F. Land (eds), *The Social Study of Information and Communication Technology*. Oxford: Oxford University Press.

Hanseth, O. and Ciborra, C. U. (eds) (2007). *Risk, Complexity and ICT*. Cheltenham: Elgar.

Hasselbladh, H. and Kallinikos, J. (2000). 'The Project of Rationalization: A Critique and Re-appraisal of Neo-institutionalism in Organization Studies', *Organization Studies*, 21/4: 697–720

Haugeland, J. (ed.) (1981). *Mind Design*. Cambridge. Mass: The MIT Press.

Hayles, C. (1999). *How we Became Posthuman: Virtual Bodies in Cybernetics, Literature, and Informatics*. Chicago: The University of Chicago Press.

Hayles, C. (2002). *Writing Machines*. Cambridge, Mass: The MIT Press.

Hayles, C. (2005). 'Computing the Human', *Theory, Culture and Society*, 22/1: 131–51.

Hayles, C. (2006). 'Unfinished Work: From Cyborg to Cognisphere', *Theory, Culture and Society*, 23/7–8: 159–66.

Hedlund, G. (1986). 'The Hypermodern MNC-A Heterarchy?', *Human Resource Management*, 25/1: 9–25.

Heidegger, M. (1971). *On the Way to Language*. New York: Harper.

Heidegger, M. (1977). *The Question Concerning Technology and Other Essays*. New York: Harper & Row.

Hopwood, A. G. (1987). 'The Archeology of Accounting Systems', *Accounting, Organizations and Society*, 12/3: 207–34.

Hoskin, K. W. and Macve, R. H. (1986). 'Accounting and the Examination: A Genealogy of Disciplinary Power', *Accounting, Organizations and Society*, 11/2: 105–36.

Hughes, T. P. (1987). 'The Evolution of Large Technological Systems', in W. E. Bijker, T. P. Hughes and T. Pinch (eds), *The social Construction of Technological Systems*, Cambridge, Mass: The MIT Press, 51–82.

Introna, L. and Nissenbaum, H. (2000). 'Shaping the Web: Why the Politics of Search Engines Matters', *Information Society*, 16(3): 169–85.

Introna, L. D. and Whitley E. D. (2000). 'About Experiments and Style: A Critique of Laboratory Research in Information Systems', *Information Technology and People*, 13/3: 161–73.

Iannacci, F. (2010). 'When is an Information Infrastructure? Investigating the Emergence of Public Sector Information Infrastructures', *European Journal of Information Systems*, 19/1: 35–48.

James, W. (2000). *Pragmatism and other Writings*. London: Penguin.

Jenkins, H. (2006). *Convergence Culture: Where New and Old Media Collide*. New York: New York University Press.

Johnson, D. J. and Nissenbaum, H. (eds) (1995). *Computers, Ethics and Social Values*, Englewood Cliffs, NJ: Prentice-Hall.

Kallinikos, J. (1992). 'The Significations of Machines', *Scandinavian Journal of Management*, 8/1: 113–32.

Kallinikos, J. (1995). 'The Architecture of the Invisible: Technology is Representation', *Organization*, 2/1: 117–40.

Kallinikos, J. (1996). *Technology and Society: Interdisciplinary Studies in Formal Organization*. Munich: Accedo.

Kallinikos, J. (1998). 'Organized Complexity: Posthumanist Remarks on the Technologizing of Intelligence', *Organization*, 5/3: 371–96.

Kallinikos, J. (2002). 'Re-opening the Black Box of Technology: Artifacts and Human agency', *23rd International Conference in Information Systems*: 287–94, Barcelona, 14–16 December.

Kallinikos, J. (2004a). 'The Social Foundations of the Bureaucratic Order', *Organization*, 11/1: 13–36.

Kallinikos, J. (2004b). 'Deconstructing Information Packages: Organizational and Behavioural Implications of ERP Systems', *Information Technology and People*, 17/1: 8–30.

Kallinikos, J. (2004c). 'Farewell to Constructivism: Technology and Context-Embedded Action', in C. Avgerou, C. Ciborra and F. Land (eds), *The Social Study of Information and Communication Technology*. Oxford: Oxford University Press.

Kallinikos, J. (2005). 'The Order of Technology: Complexity and Control in a Connected World', *Information and Organization*, 15: 185–202.

Kallinikos, J. (2006). *The Consequences of Information: Institutional Implications of Technological Change*. Cheltenham: Edward Elgar.

Kallinikos, J. (2009a). 'On the Computational Rendition of Reality', *Organization*, 16/2: 183–202.

Kallinikos, J. (2009b). 'The Making of Ephemeria: On the Shortening Life Spans of Information', *The International Journal of Interdisciplinary Social Sciences*, 4/3: 227–36.

Kallinikos, J. (2009c). 'D'un soi émietté. Remarques sur la technologie et l'individualité', (Precarious Selves: Remarks on Technology and Individuality), *Cités* 39: 13–26 (Special Issue on Control Societies).

Kallinikos, J. (2010). 'The "Age of the Smart Machine": A 21st Century View', *Encyclopedia of Software Engineering*, New York: Taylor and Francis (forthcoming, December 2010).

Kallinikos, J., Aaltonen, A. and Marton, A. (2010). 'A Theory of Digital Objects', *First Monday*, 15: 6–7, June.

Kallinikos, J. and Hasselbladh, H., (2009). 'Work, Control and Computation: Rethinking the Legacy of Neo-Institutionalism', *Research in the Sociology of Organizations*, vol. 27: 257–82.

Kallinikos, J., Hasselbladh, H. and Marton. A. (2010). 'Governing Social Practice: Technology versus Institutions', *26th EGOS Colloquium*, Lisbon, 1–4 July.

Kallinikos, J. and Mariategui, J-C. (2008). 'Media Convergence and Organizational Change: Video Production and Distribution in the Age of the Internet', *24th EGOS Colloquium*, Amsterdam, 9–11 July.

Kaptelinin, V. and Nardi, B. (2006). *Acting with Technology*. Cambridge, Mass: The MIT Press.

Kling, R. (1992). 'When Gunfire Shatters Bone: Reducing Sociotechnical Systems to Social Relations', *Science, Technology and Human Values*, 17/3: 381–5.

Kling, R. (1996). *Computerization and Controversy*. San Diego: Academic Press.

Knights, D., Noble, F., Vurdubakis, T. & Willmott, H. (2002). 'Allegories of Creative Destruction: Technology and Organization in Narratives of the e-Economy', in S. Woolgar (ed.), *Virtual Society? Technology, Hyperbole, Reality*. Oxford: Oxford University Press.

Knorr-Cetina, K. and Bruegger, U. (2002). 'Global Microstructures: The Virtual Societies of Financial Markets', *American Journal of Sociology*, 107/4: 905–50.

Koch, C. (2004). 'Innovation Networking between Stability and Political Dynamics', *Technovation*, 24/9: 729–39.

Krumbholz, M., Galliers, J., Coulianos, N. and Maiden N. A. M. (2000). 'Implementing Enterprise Resource Planning Packages in Different Corporate and National Cultures', *Journal of Information Technology*, 15/4: 267–80.

Kumar, V., Maheshwari, B. and Kumar, U. (2003). 'An Investigation of Critical Management Issues in ERP Implementation: Empirical Evidence from Canadian Organizations', *Technovation*, 23 (2003): 793–807.

Kumar, K. and Van Hillegersberg, J. (2000). 'ERP Experiences and Evolution', *Communications of the ACM*, 43/4: 23–6, April 2000.

Lackoff, G. (1995). 'Body, Brain and Communication', in J. Brook & I. A. Boal (eds), *Resisting the Virtual Life*. San Francisco: City Lights.

Lamb, R. and Kling, R. (2003). 'Reconceptualizing Users as Social Actors in Information Systems Research', *MIS Quarterly*, 27/2: 197–235.

Lanzara, G. F. (2009). 'Reshaping Practice Across Media: Material Mediation, Medium Specificity and Practical Knowledge in Judicial Work', *Organization Studies*, 30/12: 1369–90.

Lanzara, G. F. (2010). 'Remediation of Practice: How Media Change the Ways We See and Do Things in Practical Domains', *First Monday*, 15/6–7, June.

Leach, E. (1976). *Culture and Communication: The Logic by which Symbols Are Connected*. Cambridge: Cambridge University Press.

Lee, Z. and Lee, J. (2000). 'An ERP Implementation Study form a Knowledge Transfer Perspective', *Journal of Information Technology*, 15/4: 281–8.

Lessig, L. (1999). *Code and other Laws of the Cyberspace*. New York: Basic Books.

Lessig, L. (2002). *The Future of Ideas: The Fate of Commons in a Connected World*. New York: Vintage.

Lessig, L. (2006). *Code: Version 2.0*. New York: Basic Books and http://pdf.codev2.cc/Lessig-Codev2.pdf. Accessed 20 August 2010.

Lilley, S., Lightfoot, G. and Amaral, P. (2004). *Representing Organization*. Oxford: Oxford University Press.

Lindblom, C. (1981). 'Comments on Decisions on Organizations', in A. Van de Ven and W. Joyce (eds), *Perspectives in Organizational Design and Behavior*. New York: Wiley.

Luhmann, N. (1993). *The Sociology of Risk*. Berlin: de Gruyter.

Luhmann, N. (1995). *Social Systems*. Stanford: Stanford University Press.

Manovich, L. (2001). *The Language of New Media*. Cambridge, Mass: The MIT Press.

Manovich, L. (2010). *Information Aesthetics*. London: Bloomsbury Academic.

March, J. G. (1988). *Decisions in Organizations*. New York: Free Press.

March, J. G. (1991). 'Exploitation and Exploration in Organizational Learning', *Organization Science'*, 2/1: 71–87.

March, J. G. & Olsen, J. P. (eds) (1976). *Ambiguity and Choice in Organizations*. Oslo: Universitetsförlaget.

March, J. G. and Olsen, J. P. (1989). *Rediscovering Institutions*. London: Free Press.

March, J. and Simon, H. (1958/1993). *Organizations*. New York: Free Press, Second Edition.

Markus, L. M, Tanis, C. Van Fenema, P. (2000). 'Multisite ERP Implementations', *Communications of the ACM*, 43/4: 42–6, April 2000.

Markus, L. M., Axline, S., Petrie, D. & Tanis, S. C. (2000) 'Learning from Adopters' Experiences with ERP: Problems Encountered and Success Achieved', *Journal of Information Technology*, 15/4: 245–65.

Marton, A. (2009). 'Self-Referential Technology and the Growth of Information. From Techniques to Technology to the Technology of Technology', *Soziale Systeme*, 15/1: 137–59.

McArthur, T. (1986). *Worlds of Reference: Lexicography, Learning and Language from the Clay Tablet to Computer*. Cambridge: Cambridge University Press.

Miller, P. and O'Leary, T. (1987). 'Accounting and the Construction of the Governable Person', *Accounting, Organizations and Society*, 12/2: 235–65.

Miller, P. and O'Leary, T. (1994). 'The Factory as Laboratory', in M. Power (ed.), *Accounting and Science*. Cambridge: Cambridge University Press.

Mintzberg, H. (1979). *The Structuring of Organizations*. Englewood Cliffs, NJ: Prentice Hall.

Mintzberg, H. (1983). *Structures in Fives*. Englewood Cliffs, NJ: Prentice Hall.

Misa, T., Brey, P. & Feenberg, A. (eds) (2003). *Modernity and Technology*. Cambridge, Mass: The MIT Press.

Moon, Y. B. (2007). 'Enterprise Resource Planning (ERP): A Review of the Literature', *International Journal of Management and Enterprise Development*, 4/3: 235–64.

Morville, P. (2005). *Ambient Findability*. Cambridge: O'Reilly.

Mumford, L. (1934). *Technics and Civilization*. San Diego, CA: HBJ.

Mumford, L. (1952). *Arts and Technics*. New York: Columbia University Press.

Mumford, L. (1970). *The Myth of the Machine: The Pentagon of Power*. New York: Columbia University Press.

Nardi, B. and Kallinikos, J. (2007). 'Opening the Black Box of Digital Technologies: Mods in World of Warcraft', *23rd EGOS Colloquium*, 5–7 July 2007, Vienna.

Nardi, B. and Kallinikos, J. (2010). 'Technology, Agency and Community: The Case of Modding in World of Warcraft', in J. Holmstrom, M. Wiberg and A. Lund (eds), *Industrial Informatics Design, Use and Innovation: Perspectives and Services*, New York: Information Science Reference (IGI Global).

Nardi, B. and Kow, Y. M. (2010). 'Digital Imaginaries: What We (Think We) Know about Chinese Gold Farming', *First Monday*, 15: 6–7, June.

Nelson, R. R. and Winter, S. G. (1982). *An Evolutionary Theory of Economic Change*. Cambridge, Mass: Harvard University Press.

Newell, A. and Simon, H. A. (1981). 'Computer Science as an Empirical Inquiry: Symbols and Search', in J. Haugeland (ed.), *Mind Design*, Cambridge: Mass The MIT Press.

Noble, D. (1984). *Forces of Production: A Social History of Industrial Automation*. New York: Alfred, A. Knopf.

Noble, D. (1985). 'Social Choice in Machine Design: The Case of Automatically Controlled Machine Tools', in D. MacKenzie and J. Wajcman (eds), *The Social Shaping of Technology*. Milton Keynes: Open University Press.

Nonaka, I. (1994). 'A Dynamic Theory of Organizational Knowledge Creation, *Organization Science*', 5/1: 14–37.

Norman, D. A. (1999). *The Invisible Computer*. London: The MIT Press.

O'Leary, D. E. (2000). *Enterprise Resource Planning Systems: Systems, Life Cycle, Electronic Commerce, and Risk*. Cambridge: Cambridge University Press.

Olsen, J. P. (2005). 'Maybe It Is Time to Rediscover Bureaucracy', *Journal of Public Administration Research and Theory*, 16: 1–24.

Ong, W. J. (1982). *Orality and Literacy. The Technologizing of the Word*. London: Routledge.

Orlikowski, W. J. (1992). 'The Duality of Technology: Rethinking the Concept of Technology in Organizations', *Organization Science*, 3/3: 398–427.

Orlikowski, W. J. (2000). 'Using Technology and Constituting Structures: A Practice Lens for Studying Technology in Organizations', *Organization Science*, 11/4: 404–28.

Orlikowski, W. J. (2007). 'Sociomaterial Practices: Exploring Technology at Work', *Organization Studies*, 28/9: 1435–48.

Ouchi, W. G. (1979). 'A Conceptual Framework for the Design of Organizational Control Mechanisms', *Management Science*, 25/9: 833–48.

Ouchi, W. G. (1980). 'Markets, Bureaucracies and Clans', *Administrative Science Quarterly*, 25/1: 129–41.

Parr, A. and Schanks, G. (2000). 'A Model of ERP Project Implementation, *Journal of Information Technology*', 15/4: 289–304.

Pentland, B. T. and Feldman, M. S. (2005). 'Organizational Routines as a Unit of Analysis', *Industrial and Corporate Change*, 14/5: 793–815.

Perrow, C. (1967). 'A Framework for the Comparative Analysis of Organizations', *American Sociological Review*, 32/2: 194–208.

Perrow, C. (1984). *Normal Accidents: Living with High Risk Technologies*. New York: Basic Books.

Perrow, C. (1986). *Complex Organizations*. New York: Random House, third edition.

Pinch, T. (2008). 'Technology and Institutions: Living in a Material World', *Theory & Society*, 37: 461–83.

Pollock, N and Williams, R. (2009). *Software and Organizations: The Biography of the Enterprise-Wide System or How SAP Conquered the World*. London: Routledge.

Pollock, N., Williams, R. and D'Adderio, L. (2007). 'Global Software and its Provenance: Generification Work in the Production of Organizational Software Packages', *Social Studies of Science*, 37: 254–80.

Pollock, N., Williams, R. and Procter, R. (2003). 'Fitting Standard Software Packages to Non-Standard Organizations: The Biography of an Enterprise-Wide System', *Technology Analysis and Strategic Management*, 15/3: 317–332.

Poster, M. (1990). *The Mode of Information*. Cambridge: Polity Press.

Poster, M. (2006). *Information Please: Culture and Politics in the Information Age*. Durham: Duke University Press.

Ptak, C. A. and Schragenheim, E. (2000). *ERP: Tools, Techniques and Applications for Integrating the Supply Chain*. London: St. Lucie Press/APICS Series on Resource Management.

Quattrone, P. and Hopper, T. (2006). 'What is *IT*: SAP, Accounting and Visibility in a Multinational Corporation', *Information and Organization*, 16/3: 212–50.

Rehn, O. (1998). 'Three Decades of Risk', *Journal of Risk Research*, 1(1), 49–71.

Ricoeur, P. (1977). *The Rule of Metaphor: Multidisciplinary Studies in the Creation of Meaning in Language*. Toronto: Toronto University Press.

Ricoeur, P. (1984). *Memory, History, Forgetting*. Chicago: The University of Chicago Press.

Rose, J. and Jones, M. (2005). 'The Double Dance of Agency: A Socio-Theoretic Account of How Machines and Humans Interact', *Systems, Signs and Actions*, 1/1: 19–37.

Runde, J., Jones, M., Munir, K. and Nikolychuk, L. (2009). 'On Technological Objects and the Adoption of Technological Product Innovations: Rules, Routines and the

Transition from Analogue Photography to Digital Imaging', *Cambridge Journal of Economics*, 33/1: 1–24.

Ryle, G. (1949). *The Concept of Mind*. New York: Barnes and Noble.

Sarlo, B. (1993). Jorge Luis Borges: *A Writer on the Edge*. London: Verso.

Sassen, S. (2004). 'Towards a Sociology of Information Technology', in C. Avgerou, C. Ciborra & F. Land (eds), *The Social Study of Information and Communication Technology*. Oxford: Oxford University Press.

Sawyer, S and Southwick, R. (2002). 'Temporal Issues in Information and Communication Technology-Enables Organizational Change: Evidence From an Enterprise Systems Implementation', *Information Society*, 18: 263–80.

Schatzki, T. R., Knorr-Cetina, K. and Von Savingy, E. (2001). *The Practice Turn in Contemporary Theory*. London: Routledge.

Schmidt, A. (2007). 'ICT and the Judiciary in the Netherlands-A State of Affairs', *Computer Law and Security*, Rep. (2007), doi: 10.1016/j.clsr.2007.03.006.

Searle, J. R. (1995). *The Construction of Social Reality*. London: Penguin.

Searle, J. R. (2010) *Making the Social World: The Structure of Human Civilization*. Oxford: Oxford University Press.

Simon, H. A. (1969). *The Sciences of the Artificial*. Cambridge, Mass: The MIT Press.

Simon, H. A. (1977). *The New Science of Management Decisions*. Englewood Cliffs: Prentice Hall.

Sinha, K. K. and Van de Ven, A. (2005). 'Designing Work Within and Between Organizations', *Organization Science*, 16/4: 389–408.

Soh, C., Kien, S. S. and Tay-Yap, J. (2000). 'Cultural Fits and Misfits: Is ERP a Universal Solution?', *Communications of the ACM*, 43/4: 47–51, April 2000.

Sontag, S. (1979). *On Photography*. London: Penguin.

Sotto, R. (1990). *Man Without Knowledge: Actors and Spectators in Organizations*, Ph. D. thesis. Stockholm: School of Business: Stockholm University.

Sotto, R. (1996). 'The Virtual Link', *Scandinavian Journal of Management*, 12/1: 25–47.

Sprott, D. (2000). 'Componentizing the Enterprise Application Packages', *Communications of the ACM*, 43/4: 63–9, April 2000.

Star, S. L and Ruhleder, K. (1994). 'Steps Towards an Ecology of Infrastructure', *CSCW*, 10: 253–64.

Strathern, M. (2002). 'Abstraction and Decontextualization: An Anthropological Comment', in S. Woolgar (ed.), *Virtual Society? Technology, Hyperbole, Reality*. Oxford: Oxford University Press.

Styhre, A. (2008). *Perception and Organization*. Houndmills: Palgrave Macmillan.

Suchman, L. (1996). 'Articulation Work', in R. Kling (ed.), *Computerization and Controversy*, San Diego: Academic Press.

Suchman, L. (2007). *Human-Machine Configurations, Second Enlarged Edition of Plans and Situated Actions*. Cambridge: Cambridge University Press.

Tapscott, D. and Williams, A. D. (2007). *Wikinomics: How Mass Collaboration Changes Everything*. London: Atlantic Books.

Terzidis, K. (2006). *Algorithmic Architecture*. London: Elsevier.

The Economist (2010). 'The Data Deluge', February 27th–March 5th 2010.

Thompson, J. D. (1967). *Organizations in Action*. New York: McGraw Hill.

Thornton, P. (2004). *Markets from Culture: Institutional Logics and Organizational Decisions*. Stanford: Stanford University Press.

Townley, B. (1994). *Reframing Human Resource Management*. London: Sage.

Tsivacou, I. (2003). *Flexibility and Boundaries in Social Systems*. Athens: Nefeli (in Greek).

Turkle, S. (1995). *Life on the Screen. Identity in the Age of the Internet*. New York: Simon & Schuster.

Valéry, P. (1989). *Dialogues*. Princeton, N. J: Princeton University Press. Originally published in France in 1921.

Voutsina, K., Kallinikos, J. and Sorensen, K. (2007). 'Codification and Transferability of IT Knowledge', *Proceedings of the 15th European Conference of Information Systems*, St: Gallen, Switzerland.

Wagner, E. L., Scott, S. V. and Galliers, R. D. (2006). 'The Creation of "Best Practice" Software', *Information and Organization*, 16/3: 251–75.

Walsham, G. (1993). *Interpreting Information Systems in Organizations*. New Work: Wiley.

Weber, M. (1947). *The Theory of Economic and Social Organization*. London: Free Press.

Weick, K. E. (1976). 'Education Organizations as Loosely-Coupled Systems', *Administrative Science Quarterly*, 21(1): 1–19.

Weick, K. E. (1979a). *The Social Psychology of Organizing*. Reading, Mass: Addison-Wesley.

Weick, K. E. (1979b). 'Cognitive Processes in Organizations', in B. M. Staw (ed.), *Research in Organizational Behavior*. London: JAI Press.

Weick, K. E. (1985). 'Cosmos versus Chaos: Sense and Nonsense in Electronic Contexts', *Organizational Dynamics*, 15: 51–64.

Weick, K. E. (1993). 'The Collapse of Sensemaking in Organizations: The Mann Gulch Disaster', *Administrative Science Quarterly*, 38: 628–52.

Weinberger, D. (2007). *Everything is Miscellaneous: The Power of the New Digital Disorder*. New York: Time Books.

Wertsch, J. W. (1991). *Voices of the Mind: A Sociocultural Approach to Mediated Action*. London: Harvester.

Wigand, R., Picot, A. and Reichwald, R. (1997). *Information, Organization and Management*, New York: Wiley.

Winner, L. (1977). *Autonomous Technology. Technics-out of Ccontrol as a Theme in Political Thought*. Cambridge, Mass: The MIT Press.

Winner, L. (1986). *The Whale and the Reactor. A Search of Limits in the Age of High Technology*. Chicago: The University of Chicago Press.

Winner, L. (1993). 'Upon opening the Black Box and Finding it Empty: Social Constructivism and the Philosophy of Technology', *Science, Technology and Social Values*, 18: 362–78.

Winner, L. (2001). 'Where Technological Determinism Went', in S. Cutcliffe and C. Mitcham (eds), *Visions of STS: Counterpoints in Science, Technology and Society Studies*. New York: State University of New York.

Winnicott, D. W. (1971). *Playing and Reality*. London: Tavistock.

Winograd, T. (1990). 'Thinking Machines. Can There Be? Are We?', in D. Partridge and Y. Wilks (eds), *The Foundations of Artificial Intelligence*. Cambridge: Cambridge University Press.

Winston, B. (1998). *Media Technology and Society*. London: Routledge.

Woolgar, S. (ed.) (2002). *Virtual Society? Technology, Hyperbole, Reality.* Oxford: Oxford University Press.

Yates, J. (1989). *Control through Communication: The Rising of System in American Management.* Baltimore: John Hopkins University.

Zittrain, J. L. (2007). 'The Generative Internet', *Harvard Law Review*, 119: 1974–2040.

Zittrain, J. L. (2008). *The Future of the Internet and How to Stop it.* London: Penguin.

Zuboff, S. (1988). *In the Age of the Smart Machine.* New York: Basic Books.

Zuboff, S. (1996). 'Foreword: The Emperor's New Clothes', in C. U. Ciborra (ed.), *Groupware and Teamwork.* New York: Wiley.

Zuboff, S. and Maxmin, J. (2003). *The Support Economy.* London: Allen Lane.

Author Index

Subject Index